Rachel Rosetti

WILD HORSES

WILD HORSES

ELWYN HARTLEY EDWARDS

HYLAS
PUBLISHING

HYLAS PUBLISHING

Publisher Sean Moore
Creative Director Karen Prince

First published by
Hylas Publishing
129 Main Street, Irvington,
New York 10533

Designed and produced by

studio cactus ltd

13 SOUTHGATE STREET WINCHESTER HAMPSHIRE SO23 9DZ UK
TEL 00 44 1962 878600 **FAX** 00 44 1962 859278
E-MAIL MAIL@STUDIOCACTUS.CO.UK **WEBSITE** WWW.STUDIOCACTUS.CO.UK

Design Sharon Moore, Laura Watson
Editorial Elizabeth Mallard-Shaw

First American Edition published in 2003

02 03 04 05 10 9 8 7 6 5 4 3 2 1

ISBN 1-59258-019-X

Printed and bound in England by Butler & Tanner Ltd
Color origination by Radstock Reproductions Ltd,
Midsomer Norton, UK

Distributed by St. Martin's Press

CONTENTS

INTRODUCTION

The decline in the world's wild horse population began some 6,000 years ago when nomadic tribes of the Eurasian steppes were responsible for the early domestication of horses. Since then the process has accelerated rapidly, and there are now no truly wild horses left anywhere on earth. The species Equus still exists in semiferal conditions but only the zebras and the asses of the wilderness have no dependence on man.

INTRODUCTION

The evolution of the "true" horse, named *Equus caballus*, was accomplished a million years ago as the culmination of an evolutionary process extending over 60 millennia. It began with a small, multitoed creature about the size of a fox, which scientists call *Eohippus*, the Dawn Horse.

The evolution of all living creatures is governed very largely by what has been termed the process of natural selection, which is taken to imply the survival of the fittest; this really means the survival of those best fitted to adapt to altered circumstances. The giant, flightless birds and the gargantuan mammals of the Cenozoic era were for one reason or another unable to adapt to new life conditions and disappeared in what, in a long hindsight, were evolutionary blind alleys. Without doubt, there were numerous contemporary relatives of *Eohippus*

About 6 million years ago, the prototype for *Equus* emerged.

that became extinct for the same reason, but *Eohippus* did adapt. It evolved, over more than 20 million years, to enter into the Miocene epoch (about 2.4–5.5 million years ago) and a time of radical change. In the intervening millennia the descendants of *Eohippus* adapted to the slowly changing environment in which forest-type vegetation gave way to savannah supporting wiry grasses. This necessitated a change from browsing to grazing, which in turn required the development of a more complex dentition, capable of a stronger, chopping action. The eyes and the shape of the head altered to give better all-round vision, suited first to a woodland and then to a plains, or steppe, environment. Proportionately, the limbs grew longer and powerful leg ligaments developed to give a long stride and more speed. Importantly, the foot structure changed to meet the requirement of a different terrain. Gradually, the multiple toes of *Eohippus* became less evident. *Merychippus*, the horse of the middle and upper Miocene epoch, still had three toes but, increasingly, the weight was carried on the central toe. Its neck was longer, to make grazing easier, and incisor teeth had formed to improve the chopping action still further.

By about 6 million years ago, a single-hoofed animal, recognizable as a horse, had become established on the North American continent. This animal was called *Pliohippus*, the ancestor of *Equus* and of the subgeneric groups of zebras, asses and hemionids (the "half-asses"), which came 5 million years later. *Pliohippus* was larger than *Merychippus*, about 12hh. (122cm), and there were probably specimens larger than that. In a variety of forms these single-hoofed horses spread over the connecting landbridges into Asia, South America, Europe and Africa. Towards the end of the ice age, about 9,000 BC, the receding ice sheets swept away those landbridges, isolating the

American continent. For reasons that have yet to be established, the horse became extinct in the Americas some 8,000 years ago. The species was not re-established until the arrival of the Spanish *conquistadores* of the 16th century, who brought horses with them for the conquest of Mexico. The development of *Equus* was left to continue in the Old World, where three principal forms of horse became established in Europe and Western Asia. Asses and zebras inhabited the north and south of Africa, respectively, while onager were centered on the Middle East.

The horses domesticated on the Eurasian steppes were the wild descendants of the three "primitive" forms of horse, which are examined in The Primitive Connection chapter (*see* p.26). What is certain is that the decline of the wild horses began from the moment of the first domestication somewhere on the wide steppes of Eurasia about 6,000 years ago. Today, there are still some horses running wild, but only the zebras and the asses of the wilderness have no dependence on man.

EQUUS CABALLUS The horses of the Camargue have been indigenous to the Rhône delta from prehistory. The 50,000-year-old bones found at Solutre may be those of the Camargue's ancestors, while cave drawings at Lascaux and Niaux (*c.*15,000 BC) bear a strong resemblance to the breed.

THE ASIATIC WILD HORSE
(Przewalski's Horse), the
Abraham of the world's
breeds, survives in its
original form, although
almost entirely in zoos
or wildlife reserves.

CREATURE OF INSTINCT

Unlike the human being, who has the ability to reason, the horse is motivated almost entirely by instincts acquired in the wild over millions of years. As a grazing animal it developed a defense system against carnivorous predators based on early detection through heightened senses of hearing, sight, and smell, and the ability to take swift, instinctive flight from perceived danger. Those instincts formed in the wild still govern the behavioral pattern of the domestic horse.

CREATURE OF INSTINCT

The physical changes that took place during the horse's evolution certainly facilitated increased intake of food and the ability to range over large areas to find fresh and more abundant plant growth. But, just as critical to the survival of any herbivorous animal, was the development of an all-round system of defense against attack by predatory carnivores, for which the horse herds and other grazing animals were natural prey.

For the grazing animal, a defense system based on detection of predators and swift flight is essential.

THE DEFENSE SYSTEM

From the beginning, defensive and physical development were interdependent, the two progressing hand in hand. Defense for *Eohippus* was a matter of concealment in the thick forest habitat in which it lived, and to make discovery even more difficult the coat pattern camouflaged the animal very effectively, breaking the outline and blending with the background. The coat, which experts think would have been similar in texture to that of a deer, would have been marked with lighter colored spots, blotches, or, possibly, stripes.

The metamorphosis from jungle browser to plains-dwelling animal demanded a radical switch in emphasis from concealment to a defense system based on detection of predators (through a highly sensitive early-warning mechanism) followed by swift, instinctive flight.

Like humans, the horse has five senses, of which smell, sight, and hearing form part of the defensive mechanism as well as playing an essential role in social contact within the herd. These are all finely tuned and highly developed, far more so than the human equivalents. Horses have a keen sense of smell, and both touch and taste have a special place in herd relationships, but it is sight and hearing that are in the forefront of the defense mechanism. The large eyes, positioned far back in the head, allow an all-round field of vision and the ability to detect the approach of a possible predator from any direction. This undeniable advantage is, however, offset by the animal's inability to focus, or to focus in the same way as human eyes do. Horses need to raise the head to focus on a distant object. The further away the object the greater will be the degree of elevation required. Large eyes are usually associated with nocturnal animals, which have good night vision. The horse is not nocturnal, but there is ample evidence to show that it sees well in the dark.

Hearing is especially acute; the structure of the head acts as a virtual sound-box. No less than thirteen pairs of muscles control the movement of the ears. Indeed, they are so mobile that they can be rotated through virtually 360 degrees to pick up sounds from any direction.

Once danger, real or imagined, is detected the defense mechanism shifts instinctively into the flight mode, the long legs allowing for escape at speed. By nature the horse is highly strung and hypersensitive in many respects; certainly in the domestic state it detects and reacts to the mood and attitude of its handlers. There are numerous instances of horses demonstrating an almost inexplicable perception, and it has to be presumed that a sixth sense, adding to the heightened awareness, plays a part in the defense system.

EYE POSTIION Because of the positioning of the eyes the horse has what amounts to all-round vision, but for that reason has to raise the head to focus on distant objects.

CONCEALMENT Coat patterns such as the zebra's stripes are a form of camouflage, which played an important part in the early horse's defense system.

In the domesticated horse intelligent handling and training that takes account of the animal's limitations may subdue the natural instincts and characteristics to a small degree, but they can never be eliminated entirely.

THE HERD SOCIETY

Central to the horse's character is the herd, which in every sense exerts an almost gravitational pull. It is, moreover, the basis of the defense system, providing corporate and individual security. Even in domestication the herd instinct is still a major influence. Horses will always seek to return to their companions, and even a horse kept on its own will always evince pleasure and even eagerness in being returned to its stable, which, in the absence of the herd, represents its centre of security. In training a horse to jump, for example, it is always a wise practice to ask it to jump fences on a track that takes it back to its companions or, in their absence, to its stable. Given that incentive the horse is likely to jump with far more enthusiasm. There are numerous other instances that illustrate the strength of attachment to the herd. On more than one occasion a cavalry trooper ordered to leave the ranks to convey a message to a neighboring formation, for instance, has been unable to comply because of his horse's refusal to leave the ranks—and the herd!

In the wild, the horse's principal preoccupation is with finding food.

It would be a fallacious simplification to suggest the complete subservience of the herd to one dominant stallion, although there will be occasions when he assumes a dominant, protective role and he is, of course, predominant in the mating season. Fights between stallions do occur but they rarely result in death or serious injury. In practice, both in wild and domestic herds, the herd will generally divide into groups, often consisting of related animals, and each group will quickly establish an order of precedence. Usually, the group leader is an older mare, well able to control the boisterous behavior of young colts. While stallions are nearly always dominant in character, it would be wrong to think of mares as necessarily submissive. Many mares have powerful personalities and can be very dominant. Conversely, while geldings may retain dominant features in domestication, many will be submissive by nature.

In the wild the principal preoccupation is with food, and the herd moves slowly from one grazing ground to the next. Every so often youngsters will indulge in play, chasing each other and generally letting off steam. The whole herd does not gallop unless it is alarmed by the perception of imminent danger.

EATING Food is a paramount preoccupation but, even when grazing, horses have a field of all-round vision and never switch off the inbuilt defence system.

At certain times of the year the reproductive urge will be paramount and sexually oriented behavior will be more apparent. Mares usually reach puberty at between the ages of 15 and 24 months. They come into estrus (season or heat) from early spring through to autumn at regular intervals between 18 and 21 days, each heat lasting five to seven days. Mares will accept the stallion during the period of heat, showing their readiness by "flashing" the genital organ and frequently passing small quantities of urine. Mares in estrus also emit scent messages, pheromones, to attract the male horse.

Although horses are not territorial animals, stallions—during the breeding season particularly—will emphasize their dominant presence by scent-marking the area. This is done by dropping faeces and by urination. To make the message even clearer, they will frequently urinate over the faeces or urine produced by mares within a group. Stallions continually check for estrus by smelling the mare's vulva and urine. As she comes to estrus he engages in tactile stimulation, also licking the vulva and displaying flehmen, the curling back of the lips which is an accompaniment to sexual excitement. (Flehmen can, however, be provoked in both sexes by unusual smells and strong tastes.) If a mare is not ready for the attentions of the stallion she will quickly drive him off with teeth and heels.

Central to the horse's character is the herd, which in every sense exerts an almost gravitational pull.

COMMUNICATION

The language of communication is complex. There is an obvious body language and there are channels of communication through the senses, including the enigmatic sixth sense. Smell plays a particularly important part, and pheromones are constantly produced by the skin glands. Mares and foals instinctively recognize each other in this way. Similarly, groups within the herd give off a corporate odor, easily recognizable by all members of the group. Tactile signals are very evident in the relationship between mare and foal and, indeed, between group members as they indulge in obviously pleasurable mutual grooming.

In a limited way horses also communicate vocally. Squeals and grunts are usually signs of aggression or excitement. Horses snort when they see or smell something that interests them particularly. They will also snort if they sense potential danger. They whinny sometimes out of excitement but often to attract separated companions. A mare, of course, reassures her foal by whickering softly.

◀ GROOMING Mutual grooming, particularly in the area of the wither, is a commonplace form of communication and reassurance between individual members of a group.

Ears are also part of the language of communication and can indicate the animal's state of mind quite unmistakably. Pricked forward in a tense manner they indicate strong interest in a particular object. The ears are lowered and become flaccid in relaxation or when dozing, and they are then accompanied by a loose, lowered body posture and often a rested foot. Anger, aggression and irritation are expressed by ears laid back on the head, the message being strengthened by bared teeth and the animal showing the white of the eyes.

DOMESTICATION

Six thousand years ago, give or take a century or two, nomadic people of the Eurasian steppes turned towards the herding of horses, which up to that point, one must presume, they had hunted sporadically for meat and hides. These resourceful Asian nomads had acquired the basic herding techniques early in their existence, although these probably took the form of following wild or semi-wild flocks of sheep, goats, cattle and, importantly, reindeer, a migratory animal whose movement is governed by the incidence of the "reindeer moss" on which it feeds.

HERDS A tried and trusted "bell" mare leads a large group, all of which will follow her and respect her authority.

In areas supporting large horse populations—such as those of the steppelands bordering the Caspian and Black Seas, where climatic conditions can be severe—horses were the most attractive animals for herding purposes because they were in every way better equipped to find food than were smaller animals and, unlike the reindeer, the horse is not migratory. Moreover, the horse herds provided for all the basic needs of human nomadic existence. Hides and hair were converted to make tents and clothing, dung was dried to make fires, and fresh meat was available on the hoof. The mares could be milked, just as in a reindeer culture, and the milk, when fermented, used to make the fiery *kummis*, the hooch or *poteen* of later centuries and other countries, which is still imbibed with enthusiasm throughout the Asian steppelands.

> **For centuries, horse herds provided for all the basic needs of human nomadic existence.**

In time, and with greater familiarity, the possession of horses gave to the steppe people an unimagined mobility, allowing them access to the more fertile and prosperous lands outside the boundaries of the steppes. These incursions by horse-peoples against their settled neighbors were, indeed, the seeds from which in course of time there grew states and empires and whole civilizations. However, in the domestication chart the horse finishes a distance behind other animals.

Sheep were kept in domestic flocks as early as 9,000 BC and were soon followed by goats, while the dog, the natural companion and ally of carnivorous, hunting man, is thought to have shared the human life from around 12,000 BC. Nor was *Equus caballus*, the name given to the modern horse, the first of the Equidae to enter the domestic state. In the lands of the Tigris and Euphrates, where the less tractable onager was more common, that difficult creature was certainly driven to chariots, despite the problems caused by temperament and conformation, well before the horse took on that role.

It is likely that the first steppe horses to be herded were the smaller ones, which would have been less difficult to manage. In time, these groups would have come to be led by an older, steadier mare on whom the herdsman could rely. Where horses are still kept in herds, as in Argentina, for instance, the leader is often an old bell mare, i.e. she carries a bell round her neck so that her whereabouts are more easily discovered. It is very unlikely that stallions would have been included in the early steppe herds. When it was necessary to breed from a mare, she would be tied out when in season to attract the attentions of a wild stallion. This practice is still carried out in some parts of the world where wild or semi-wild stock exists. The male product of such matings would be eaten when young, before it posed behavioral problems, or would be gelded to ensure a degree of amenability. Nonetheless, geldings within a group can be a nuisance when mares are in season and it is unlikely that many would have been kept after the animals were weaned. In time, as management became more advanced, some geldings would have been used as riding animals or for the transportation of the tribe's goods and chattels. Fillies presented no such problems and would become mothers and providers of milk.

It is probable that as well as being small the early subjects of domestication would have been pretty rough specimens by modern standards and certainly not good conformational examples. To offset their appearance, however, they would have been tough and exceptionally hardy, with legs and feet of iron and the instincts of survival highly developed. Initially, however, the impact of domestication would have been retrograde rather than otherwise. Accepting the hypothesis of the deliberate selection of smaller animals on account of manageability, the ensuing stock would have been small initially. Furthermore, natural independence would decrease as the animal became more reliant on the herdsman. Some of the inbred ability to fend for itself would be lost, and the initiative to search for its own food diminished. Modern horses, for example, stabled, groomed and provided with food and usually clothing, too, would make a poor job of survival if turned out in the wild. And that is the price of domestication and the resultant loss of the wild vigor.

Modern, domesticated horses would make a poor job of survival if they were turned out to live in the wild.

THE PRIMITIVE
CONNECTION

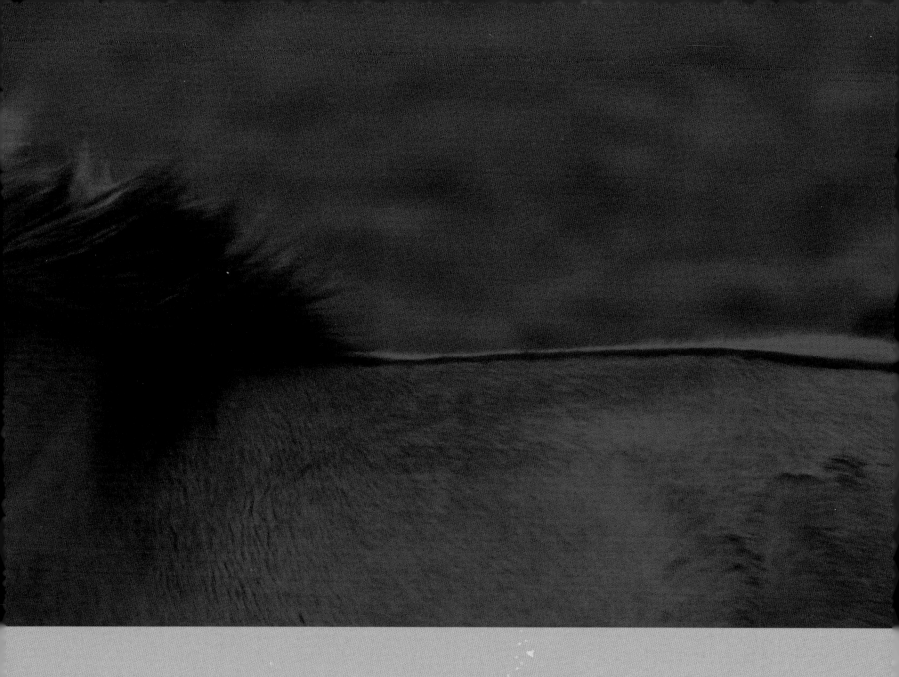

The history of the horse began some 60 million years ago, long before the emergence of Homo erectus. The "true" horse, Equus caballus, originated on the American continent about a million years ago, and the link between that and the modern horse is provided by the evolution of three primitive breeds, only one of which—the Asiatic Wild Horse of the central Asian steppes—survives in its original form.

THE PRIMITIVE CONNECTION

While there are still grey areas in establishing with accuracy the development of the horse following the appearance of *Equus*, there is broad support for the theory postulating that the origin of the modern horse can be found in three primitive types, one of which survives today after the best part of 10,000 years.

Differences in environment resulted in various forms of *Equus* existing contemporaneously in the glacial and postglacial periods. The three forms through which it is possible to trace the domestic horse are:

The modern light horse can be attributed to the Asiatic Wild Horse and its subsequent derivatives.

1. The Asiatic Wild Horse (or Przewalski's Horse), called *Taki* in Mongolia and *Kertag* by the Kirghiz people. Its full scientific title is *Equus caballus przewalskii przewalskii* Poliakov.
2. The lighter, swifter-running Tarpan (literally "wild horse"), which Professor J. Cossar Ewart of Edinburgh had designated as a "plateau" horse. Professor J. U. Duerst of Bern termed it "desert" horse, although "steppe" would be just as appropriate a word. Scientifically it is catalogued as *Equus caballus przewalskii gmelini* Antonius.
3. The Forest or Diluvial Horse, so called because it belonged to that period. It is known as *Equus caballus silvaticus* and it is the progenitor of the postglacial *Equus caballus germanicus*.

In simplistic terms the modern light horse can be attributed to the Asiatic Wild Horse and the Tarpan, their crosses and subsequent derivatives. The Forest or Diluvial Horse is thought to be responsible for the heavy draught breeds, allowing for possible crosses to the Asiatic Wild Horse and such environmental changes as might affect their development.

▶ PRZEWALSKI'S HORSE The discovery of the Asiatic Wild Horse is attributed to Col. Nicolai Przewalski, after whom it was named, although its existence was known to earlier European travelers in the region.

There is also evidence of a fourth primitive, the largely unconsidered Tundra Horse of the Arctic Circle. Its remains, it is thought, were those found alongside a cache of mammoth bones in the Yana valley of northeast Siberia, where winter temperatures fall below those at the North Pole. About this primitive there is a surprising unanimity among hippologists: in the words of Professor F. N. Zeuner, "It has almost certainly not contributed to the domestic stock of horses."

Soviet scientists, however, believe that the local, white-coated Yakut ponies are direct descendants of the extinct Tundra, and they certainly display many of the primitive characteristics, among them the dorsal stripe, zebra-barred lower limbs, and a dark lattice pattern on the shoulder. The Yakut is also able to survive in temperatures as low as 40–58°F (40–50°C) below freezing.

Of the three principal primitive horses, only the Asiatic Wild Horse survives in its original form to provide the link between the prehistoric horse and that of our own times. Most are kept in zoos and wildlife parks, but in recent years selected groups have been returned to their natural habitat in Mongolia.

THE ASIATIC WILD HORSE

The range inhabited by the Asiatic Wild Horse encompassed both the European and central Asian steppes, overlapping the territory of the Tarpan roughly along the line drawn by longitude 40. The Kirghiz people had known of the Asiatic Wild Horse's existence for generations and, indeed, had hunted it almost to extinction by the 19th century. Several European travelers had also heard reports of primitive dun-colored Mongolian horses; one of these, the English naturalist Col. Hamilton Smith, obtained detailed descriptions and published his findings in the leading natural history journal of the day, *Jardine's Naturalist's Library*, in 1814. However, it is to Nicolai Mikhailovitch Przewalski, a colonel in the army of Imperial Russia, that the discovery of the Asiatic Wild Horse is universally credited and after whom the breed is named.

Przewalski, an intrepid explorer, experienced military surveyor and cartographer, was also a valued agent of his government—like many of the Europeans, Russians, and British who penetrated deep into the inhospitable terrain of central Asia during the 19th century. They were involved in negotiations with local rulers and in providing intelligence about any military operations which, in the British view, might lead to a Russian army moving towards India. Insatiably curious, these very brave young men provided every sort of information about the people they encountered and their customs; and, since all were of a sporting turn of mind, they also made detailed studies of wildlife, including the horse and pony types which, in the event of hostilities might be a critical factor.

Przewalski, who traveled throughout Mongolia and Tibet, came across wild horse herds in the area of the Tachin Schah (the Mountains of the Yellow Horses) when he reached the edges of the Gobi Desert in 1879. He obtained a skin from the Kirghiz tribesmen and it was from this that the zoologist J. S. Poliakov made the first scientific description of the primitive horse that would later be acknowledged as the Abraham of the equine race.

Poliakov named the horse *Equus caballus przewalskii przewalskii* Poliakov (although the name is often shortened to the simpler *Equus przewalskii*). Ten years later, Russian and European zoologists and collectors, among them the Duke of Bedford, had captured sufficient wild stock to form a breeding nucleus from which the present-day complement of the wild Przewalski is descended.

Detailed studies soon revealed that the Przewalski Horse was an animal with unique characteristics. Unlike those of domestic horses, the chromosomes—which carry the genes responsible for the transmission of hereditary characteristics—number 66 rather than 64 (or 33 pairs rather than 32). In appearance the horse is very distinctive. The coat color is sand-dun with a cream-colored underbelly. The legs are black, frequently striped, or barred, like those of the zebra, and the mane and tail are similarly colored. Usually, there is a pronounced dorsal stripe, often accompanied by a cross over the shoulder.

POLISH TARPAN The last wild Tarpan was killed at Askania Nova in the Ukraine in 1879, but thereafter wild herds were "reconstituted" in Poland by careful backbreeding to Tarpan-related stock.

These primitive features, with more or less emphasis, still occur in individuals of modern breeds and are a constant reminder of the strength of the modern horse's relationship to the primitive animal. A notable primitive feature that seldom occurs in modern stock is the Przewalski's mane, which grows upright to a length of 8in (20cm), unlike that of the domestic horse (which falls to one side or the other). The texture is exceptionally harsh and there is little or no forelock. Reflecting the common root of all Equidae, which includes the asses and the zebras, the tail hairs of the Przewalski are short at the top, like those of mules and donkeys, and long and coarse on the lower half. The head is long and heavy, inclining to the convex, and with the eyes set very high and close to the ears. The hair on the muzzle and around the eyes is paler than the coat color. Very notably, the back structure is closer to being asinine than otherwise. Withers are indiscernible, and the back is straight, like that of the onager, kulan, and zebra. The height is about 13hh. (132cm).

The Asiatic Wild Horse is by nature aggressive and even fierce. It is also possessed of a peculiar "primitive vigor," which results in high fertility levels and exceptional qualities of constitution and stamina. Even in captivity the horse can never be considered tame. It is, indeed, difficult to handle and no one has ever attempted to break one to saddle or harness. This is not to say that it would be impossible, for there are instances of zebras—not the most tractable of animals—being ridden and, more particularly, driven in harness, while the onager preceded the horse in drawing chariots, albeit being controlled, like oxen, by a ring through the nose.

THE TARPAN

Just as powerfully pervasive in its influence on the development of the modern horse is the Tarpan, once to be found in large numbers all over eastern Europe and the Ukrainian steppes. It was, however, intensively hunted and did not survive in any numbers into the last part of the 18th century. Even then, the wild stock had mated extensively over a long period with domestic animals, a fact made evident in the character and appearance of many European ponies, in particular the Hucul and Konik of the Ukraine.

◀ KONIK The Konik (meaning pony or little horse) is the farm pony of Poland and a descendant of the Tarpan, which it closely resembles in character and appearance.

It is most probable, also, that the Sorraia of Portugal is of direct Tarpan descent and therefore a significant influence in the evolution of the Iberian horses. Taking the argument a stage further it is not too farfetched to see the Tarpan as the primitive lead in to the desert horses of Turkmene and to the Arabian horse itself.

The gifted zoologist Helmut Otto Antonius commented in 1922 that the Tarpan was "...of the greatest importance in connection with the origin of the domestic horse," while scientific opinion is virtually unanimous in holding the Tarpan to be of "... a type more specialized towards the horse" than towards the ass (W. Salensky, 1907).

POITEVIN France's coarse, slow-moving Poitevin, or Mulassier, is probably the nearest modern equivalent to the extinct Forest Horse of northern Europe. It was employed originally in drainage work on the Poitou marshes.

J. F. Gmelin, the Russo-German scientist, captured four wild specimens near Bobrowsk in Russia in 1768, and Antonius, Director of the Schonbrunn Zoological Garden in Vienna, catalogued the animal as *Equus caballus przewalskii gmelini* Antonius. Gmelin described the slender-legged horse, product of the dry steppe conditions of its habitat, as standing at about 13hh. (132cm), mouse-colored with prominent black points, and a "disproportionately thick" head (referring, one presumes, to the pronounced convex profile). He noted also that the ears were long, describing what today would be called lopears.

At the end of the 19th century, a decade or so after the last wild Tarpan had been killed near Askania Nova in the Ukraine in 1879, the Polish authorities undertook the task of "re-creating" the Tarpan in forest reservations at Popielno and Bialowieza. They selected animals retaining the most pronounced Tarpan character and with great skill bred back to selected, related strains to produce an animal which, on the available evidence, closely resembles the original wild horse, with the possible exception of the upright mane.

THE NEW TARPAN

The reconstituted Tarpans display the coat coloring described by Gmelin, and hair that is wiry in texture, like that of a deer. The dorsal stripe, barred legs and sometimes stripes on the body are all evident and, as with some other truly wild animals, the coat turns white in severe, winter conditions.

More importantly, the "new" Tarpan retains much of the unique primitive vigor that accounts for its influence on subsequent domestic stock. Fierce, and to all intents impossible to handle without sedation, the animals are possessed of a strength disproportionate to their size. They have exceptional powers of endurance and stamina and a constitution second to none. The fertility rate in the herds is high and abortion unknown. They do not seem to suffer from sickness of any kind, and it has been noted that any wounds heal with remarkable speed and without outside intervention.

FOREST HORSE

While the Forest Horse that existed in the marshlands of Europe a million years ago has, without doubt, been extinct for a very long time its influence is discernible in breeds like the coarse, slow-moving Poitevin, which, when put to the Poitevin jackass (or Baudet de Poitou), produce the very large and exceptionally strong mules around which a thriving export industry was built.

It is not unreasonable to suppose that the Forest Horse would have been about 15hh. (152cm), thick legged, heavy bodied, and covered in thick, coarse hair. The large feet would have been suited to the swamp environment, and the coat would have been strongly dappled to blend with the surroundings. Traces of such a horse have been found in Scandinavia and dated as being 10,000 years old, while other discoveries in northwest Germany date from a mere 3,000 years ago, but knowledge of the existence of such an animal can hardly be compared with the reality of the Asiatic Wild Horse and the replicated Tarpan.

The "new" Tarpan retains much of the unique primitive vigor

TIGER-HORSES
OF AFRICA

It is probable that a great variety of zebra ranged all over Europe, Africa, Asia, and North America up to as little as 100,000 years ago, and even less. Now the zebra is found only in southern Africa. Indiscriminate shooting in the past and the pressures of a modern environment have depleted the zebra herds, and today only three principal species of this distinctive animal survive.

TIGER-HORSES OF AFRICA

Zebras can be regarded as striped horses and are divided into two groups, or subgenera: *Dolichohippus* and *Hippotigris* (meaning tiger-horse). *Dolichohippus* is exemplified by Grevy's Zebra (*Equus grevyi*), the largest zebra, the most handsome and the most specialized. *Hippotigris* is represented by two species—the Mountain Zebra (*Equus zebra*) and Burchell's Zebra (*Equus burchelli*)—and a number of subspecies.

The pattern of stripes on all zebras is unique to each individual; the variation is greatest in the shoulder area.

Grevy's is the senior member of the trio, evolving perhaps 5 million years ago and the first to split away from the first single-toed horse, *Pliohippus*, the true horse. *Pliohippus* was the source of the whole subgeneric group encompassing zebras, domestic and wild asses, and the hemionids, the "half-asses."

What is remarkable is that at these early dates there existed two separate forms of the subgenus, both evolving in North America. They survived on that continent up to about a million years ago, when significant environmental changes were taking place. Meanwhile they had moved over into Eurasia via the landbridges of the Bering Strait.

Three million years ago zebras were spread throughout Europe and existed there up to 100,000 years ago. Similarly, and in the same time scale, large specimens of *Dolichohippus* were to be found in central Asia, China and India. Today, the zebra family is confined to Africa. The habitat of Grevy's Zebra is in the low desert country of Kenya, Ethiopia, and Somalia; that of the Mountain Zebras in the ranges north of the Orange River and possibly, in small numbers, in a few isolated areas of the Cape Province. Burchell's Zebras, which are the most numerous, are found all over east and southeast Africa.

GREVY'S ZEBRA

Equus grevyi was named in 1882 when Jules Grevy, then President of France, was presented with a live specimen by King Menelik of Shoa (Ethiopia). Like all zebras it has longer forelegs in proportion to its frame than other Equidae, but there are also other distinctive features. Moreover it has no inter-relationship with the subgenus *Hippotigris*. It is the largest living truly wild species of equid, measuring up to 15hh. at the wither, a shade over 150cm. (although most fall between 13.1hh./135cm and 13.3hh./140cm), and weighing 880lb (400kg) and

▶ BURCHELL'S ZEBRA This zebra, often classified as the Plains Zebra, is the plump little animal seen commonly in zoos and the one most widely distributed in Africa. There are particularly large herds in the Serengeti plains.

upwards. Longlegged and of slender build it has the most spectacular stripe pattern of all zebras. The stripes are black on white and close together, there is a distinct dorsal list, and the stripes are curved round the quarters while the belly is white.

The erect mane is notably tall. The ears, too, are distinctive. They are round, prominent, and furred on the inside. The chestnuts, confined to the forelimbs (as with all zebras and asses), are particularly small, but it is the head that is noteworthy for its primitive character. It resembles very closely that of the early equids of 3–3.5 million years ago with small, thinly enameled teeth set in the primitive pattern. The gestation period of Grevy's Zebra is 390 days, which is longer than that of the horse (334 days for colts and 332.5 for fillies) and of any other zebra or ass. To mark the differences still further there is the voice of Grevy's Zebra—a hoarse grunt interspersed with a whistling noise!

MOUNTAIN ZEBRA

Without doubt the Mountain Zebra has suffered a serious and worrying decline in numbers, largely as a result of being in competition with domestic animals in its habitat. The species is divided into two subspecies: Hartmann's Zebra (*Equus zebra hartmannae*) in the north of the range and the Cape Mountain Zebra (*E. z. zebra*) in the south. The stockily built Cape is the smallest of the zebra family standing at 12hh. (120cm), while Hartmann's can be 12.3hh. (130cm). The latter is marked with narrow, widely spaced stripes on an off-white ground, while the Cape has broad black stripes, set close together and narrower feet. In both the belly is free of stripes and the facial markings are dark brown rather than black.

Mountain zebras are distinguishable from all other equids by the small, square dewlap in the middle of the throat and also by the curious hair growth along the back. From croup to withers the hair grows forwards rather than backwards. The ears in this species are long and quite unlike those of Grevy's Zebra, while the mane grows high and erect.

In an adaptation to the mountain climate the heart of the Mountain Zebra weighs 7lb (3.2kg), while that of Burchell's Zebra, whose habitat is at a lower altitude, is 4½lb (2.05kg). The larger heart enables mountain zebras to make more efficient use of the oxygen-poor mountain air.

> # The Mountain Zebra is unique among equids in having a small, square dewlap.

◀ GREVY'S ZEBRA This zebra, the largest of the subgenera, is directly connected to the early equids through the first single-toed horse, *Pliohippus*. It was named Grevy in 1882 after the French president Jules Grevy.

There is another interesting comparison with Burchell's Zebras. Burchell's herds are led by a lead mare, while the mountain herds moving single file on mountain tracks are led by the stallion. The Mountain stallion is, indeed, the more protective, constantly making use of higher ground to observe the country through which the herd is passing. He will drink last at waterholes and will take the lead in digging for water in dry riverbeds. The call of the mountain zebra has been described as a low, snuffling neigh or whinny or as a whinny followed by a "honk."

The Quagga came to the point of extinction almost by accident and almost unnoticed.

BURCHELL'S ZEBRA

Burchell's Zebra (*Equus burchelli*), sometimes called the Plains Zebra, is a plump, sleek zebra, standing on short legs. It is usually between 12–12.3hh. (120–130cm). There is some variation in the coat coloration between the zebras in one area and those in another, but there is a discernible basic pattern characterized by horizontal stripes on the haunches. Burchell's Zebra, for no valid reason it would seem, was frequently confused or perhaps wrongly associated with the Quagga (*see* below) and, indeed, was on occasions termed "bontequagga," meaning painted quagga.

The average gestation period of this zebra is 371 days, longer than that of the horse but less than that of Grevy's Zebra. A peculiar feature of Burchell's Zebra is its overt antagonism towards the donkey: if it gets the chance, it will attack a donkey fiercely with hooves and teeth. No theory has ever been put forward to explain this propensity. The calls of Burchell's Zebras seem to be more varied than those of others belonging to the subgenus. In southern Africa there is the honking cry like that given by wild geese, while in the east a whistle and grunt combination is more noticeable.

A herd of Burchell's Zebras is composed of family groups that remain intact even when several herds graze the same area. Although zebra herds are not territorial in the sense that they will defend a specific area against other herds, they do occupy a definable home range, which they share with other herds. In the Serengeti, where the ranges are larger than in the Ngorongoro Crater, for example, the herds migrate for up to 60 miles (100km) in the dry season to larger ranges offering more waterholes. The typical habitat is open, flat plainlands well covered with ground vegetation. Zebras are less selective grazers than antelopes and will consume old, coarse grasses as well as other plant growth that antelopes will not eat. As a result, herds of both species coexist quite easily.

QUAGGA

The Quagga (*Equus burchelli quagga*), the most distinctive form of which was named *E. b. quagga danielli*, is in its original, if varied, form extinct, the last ones in Africa being shot between 1858 and 1861.

Classified as a subspecies of Burchell's Zebra, they were once numerous in the plains south of the Vaal River, in the area of the Orange River near Ramah, and in the northern highlands of Kunana district from where they would move to around Mafeking in the winter. Quaggas' Flats, along the Great Fish River, was so named because of the large herds that were once found there. The Quagga came to the point of extinction almost by accident and almost unnoticed. Farmers just went on shooting them to provide meat for their workers without ever thinking that so numerous a species could ever be destroyed entirely.

CAPE MOUNTAIN ZEBRA
This zebra is declining in numbers and is the most threatened by competition within its environment. Its heart is larger than that of Burchell's Zebra because of the mountain climate.

ZEBRA HERD A large group of zebra at an established watering place. Despite a discernible pattern there is a noticeable variation in coat coloration.

The Quagga is about 13hh. (132cm), and shares common features with both Burchell's and Mountain zebras. The difference is in the coat coloration. In general, it is only the Quagga's forehand and head that exhibit a striped pattern, the body being a light dun color and the legs almost white. The subspecies of Burchell's Zebra found in the far south of the continent (Chapman's Zebra, *E. b. antiquorum*), is usually less strongly striped and, in some, striping is no more than minimal. Specimens of this sort are the basis of the backbreeding exercise taking place at the Cape to re-create the Quagga. The cry of the Quagga—a sharp, barking noise, not unlike Burchell's "qua-ha"—is the origin of the name Quagga.

There are the occasional instances of zebras being domesticated. Mrs M. H. Hayes, wife of Capt. Horace Hayes (1842–1904), a leading veterinarian, author and horseman, rode one sidesaddle, and Lord Rothschild had a team

of Burchell's Zebras, although in a photograph of this unusual turnout it is clear that a horse has been put in as the nearside leader—in the hope, perhaps, that it would provide a steadying influence on its colorful companions. Nonetheless, zebras are not noted for their tractability and they can be savage and aggressive.

This, it would seem, was not the case with the wild Quagga (nor is it so with the modern replicated version of the Quagga, which is described as being tame). In 1826 a pair of Quaggas drew a phaeton in Hyde Park, London, and caused a sensation among the smart social set frequenting the Row. George Stubbs painted a portrait of a Quagga, and London Zoo employed a team of Quaggas in its forage cart. In fact, Quaggas were to be found in many of the European zoos. The last one in Britain died at London Zoo in 1872; and in 1883 the Quagga kept at Amsterdam's zoo also died, and the breed was pronounced extinct.

HYBRIDS

While the African zebras may sometimes form mixed herds, there is no interbreeding between the species and so there are no hybrid zebras. However, sterile hybrids can be produced using other equids, although this has usually occurred only in captivity. Zebroids, for instance, were bred commercially by Raymond Hook of Nanyuki on the edge of Mount Kenya. He used a Grevy's Zebra on horse mares, and produced foals that more closely resembled the horse parent but had tufted tails and pale, narrow striping on the face and legs. They were used as pack animals on Mount Kenya and were said to be strong and docile although dull in character.

◀ QUAGGA TYPE The Quagga in its original form is extinct, but this group of zebra show Quagga characteristics in the lack of color on quarters and legs.

ASSES OF THE WILDERNESS

Onagers or hemionids (half-asses) were used to draw chariots long before horses. They were driven from a nosering like those used for oxen. The wild ass is, indeed, a remarkable creature, capable of sustaining high speeds over long distances; it is also extremely agile. The word hemionid is used to describe an animal with the nature and some of the characteristics of both horse and ass. It is not, as might be thought, a cross between an ass and something else.

ASSES OF THE WILDERNESS

Asses are widespread, extending all over Asia, the Middle East, and North Africa. All belong to the genus *Equus* and to the subgenus *Asinus*, which can be divided into four species: African Wild Ass (*Equus africanus*), Asiatic Wild Ass, or Onager (*E. hemionus*), Kiang (*E. kiang*), and the burro, or donkey (*E. asinus*). All members of the subgenus differ from horses materially. The chestnuts, the horny callosities found on the inside of both fore and hind legs of the horse, occur only on the forelegs of the ass and zebra. In addition, asses have five rather than six lumbar vertebrae; they have long ears, an upright mane stopping short of the forelock, and a tufted tail. The back is straight, lower at the wither than at the croup, and in most species the feet are narrow, straightsided, and small—ideally suited, in fact, for the terrain over which they move. The period of gestation in the horse is around 11 months while that of the ass is 12 months. Then there is the characteristic bray, which is quite unlike the horse's neigh and whinny or, indeed, the curious grunts, barks and whistles of the zebra. G. K. Chesterton wrote of the "... monstrous head and sickening cry ..."

> **The burro, or donkey, the best known of the asses, was domesticated over 5,000 years ago—long before horses.**

The most common and best known of the asses is the burro (*E. asinus*), which has spread to most parts of the world. It was domesticated at least 5,000 years ago, well before horses were tamed for domestic usage.

> ▸ BURRO Called donkey in Britain, the burro remains a beast of burden in many parts of the world and is often shamefully abused. In Europe, however, the donkey has achieved fashionable status in the show ring, where it is driven, sometimes ridden, and competes in halter classes.

AFRICAN WILD ASS

The principal ancestor of the burro is held to be the African Wild Ass (*E. africanus*), of which there are two subspecies, the Nubian (*E. a. africanus*), which most resembles the domestic ass, and the Somali (*E. a. somalicus*). Once, both races inhabited the whole of North Africa from the Atlantic to the Indian Ocean and right up to the Mediterranean. In more recent times the effect of larger human populations and increasing economic pressures on the environment have pushed the Nubians inland to the deserts of southern Algeria. The Somali Ass is found further to the southeast, towards the Horn of Africa.

The Nubian, which measures only 12hh. (122cm) or so, is grey, taking on a reddish tinge in summer. It has no leg stripes but is distinguished by a strong shoulder cross. The Somali is larger, up to 14hh. (142cm). It is reddish-grey without either dorsal stripe or shoulder stripes, but it has zebra stripes on the legs.

The division between the Nubian and Somali asses runs through Ethiopia, where there may still be small wild herds of Somali Asses. Both races live in arid zones subject to extremes of heat, up to 122°F (50°C), and are capable of going without water for as much as two to three days. The Somali Ass, once under the protection of the Sultan of Aussa (who punished any man killing one by cutting off his hand), still survives in small numbers. Whether the position is the same with the Nubian is less certain.

SOMALIAN WILD ASS
This ass is distinctive in its coloration, the red-grey coat being without dorsal and shoulder markings but with very prominent zebra marks on the legs.

ASIATIC WILD ASS

Western Asia, in particular Mongolia and the high Tibetan plateau as well as the Indian deserts, is the habitat of the Asiatic Wild Asses (*Equus hemionus*), sometimes called onagers or hemionids (half-asses). The use of the word hemionid is confusing as it suggests a cross between an ass and something else, whereas it is meant to describe an animal that has the nature and some of the characteristics of both horse and ass.

The most notable feature of the hemionid—one that is absent in the domestic ass and in the zebra—is the extreme length of the lower limbs combined with the high croup conformation. In principle this is the conformation characterizing the cheetah and the greyhound, and it allows the animal to move at surprisingly high speeds.

Once, the deserts of Iran and Iraq supported the wild ass of the Bible, known as the Persian Onager (*E. h. onager*), which may well have spilled over into Syria. There is some confusion about the nomenclature of this subspecies, but it is almost certainly extinct in the wild, although stock is still kept at Hamburg Zoo.

The Mongolian Kulan (*E. h. hemionus*), called *Dziggetai* or *Jigetai* (longeared) by the steppe people, can reach speeds of up to 35–40mph (55–65km/h) and can easily outrun its principal animal predator, the desert wolf, which is certainly not slow. R. C. Andrews, who studied the Kulan in the Gobi Desert between 1922 and 1925, recorded the case of a stallion pursued by a car averaging 30mph (48km/h) over a distance of 16 miles (28km). Alas, its speed is less valuable in the survival stakes when pursued by hunters armed with rifles.

Highly adapted to desert living, African Wild Asses have been known to go for up to four days without water.

The Kulan varies between 12 and 13hh. (122 and 132cm) and bears a close resemblance to the horse in respect of the feet and voice. The ears, while bigger than those of horses, are smaller than those of other hemionids. The nostrils, however, are notably larger than in either horse or domestic ass and are a necessary adaptation to the habitat's high altitude and rarefied atmosphere. The coat color varies with the seasons: it is grey-white in winter and changes to sandy-red in summer. Unlike the domestic ass there is no striping over the shoulder.

Closely related to the Kulan is the Khur (*E. h. khur*), which is also called the Indian Onager or Ghor-khar. The Hindi word *ghor-khar*, or more correctly *ghoor-khur*, can be translated as "wild mule."

A hundred years ago the Khur was to be found in India's Rann of Kutch, on the western side of the subcontinent, in Gujerat itself, in the Thar and Great Indian deserts, in the Sindh desert to the north, and in Baluchistan west of the Indus. In all these areas it was shot extensively, and it is probable that it survives only in small pockets of the Rann of Kutch and the Thar Desert, and in isolated areas of Baluchistan.

Smaller than the largest of the Kulan, the Khur's coat color is a reddish yellow-grey with the dorsal stripe terminating halfway down the tail. The formation of the nasal bones is interesting, since they are raised to form a discernible bump on the face. The effect, it is suggested, is to increase the size of the nasal cavity to allow moistening of the dry, desert air before it reaches the lungs.

Despite their comparatively small stature, hemionids can run as swiftly as any equid.

Like others in the subgenus *Asinus*, the Khur is capable of sustaining high speeds, 28–30mph (45–48km/h), over long distances. The Indian naturalist E. P. Gee timed a herd of Khur traveling at that speed for over half an hour. For, despite their comparatively small stature hemionids are as fast as any of the equine races, including the Thoroughbred, and possessed of stamina and endurance in excess of the Arabian. Moreover, they have jumping ability of quite the same order as any international showjumper!

Erna Mohr, of Prague, one of the world's most respected equine authorities, recalls chasing a female Persian Onager for over three-quarters of an hour at almost 30mph (48km/h). When caught the animal was not even sweating. On the same capture expedition she saw two onagers jump a wall 7½ft (2.3m) high! Onagers are very good climbers, too. In the Badkhyz Reserve, Iran, Persian Onagers climb very steep, rough slopes on their migration routes. Climbing is assisted by the formation of hard excrescences on the outer sides of the hoof (*Horses, Asses, and Zebras*, Colin P. Groves, 1974).

▶ ONAGERS These asses were once widespread throughout Asia, and in the past substantial herds lived even on the steppe west of the Urals. Today the largest concentration of onagers is in Mongolia.

KIANG

The Kiang (*Equus kiang*) is as remarkable as any of the *Asinus* group, inhabiting the high Tibetan plateau, north of the mountain kingdoms of Bhutan, Sikkim, and Nepal, where the terrain is never below 4,000m (13,000ft) above sea level. In fact the Kiang steppe, lying below the even harsher, windswept habitat of the wild yak, rises to 4,800m (15,750ft) in its highest parts. At this altitude the plant growth can be limited to as little as two or three months a year.

To cope with the vegetation of low shrubs and the tough, sharp but highly nutritious swamp grasses, the Kiang has developed hard, thick lips and an especially horny palate. The intake of swamp grass is vital to the Kiang. It is rich in silicic acid and it allows the animals to build up reserves of body fat against the climatically severe winter months when food is sparse and lacking in nutrient value.

The Kiang herds are always led by an old mare rather than by a stallion, and it is rare for there to be any stragglers. Otherwise, they are very shy and difficult to approach, quickly taking up wheeling defensive formations if they feel threatened. The Kiang lead a largely undisturbed existence and are in no danger of being hunted by the deeply religious Tibetans, who regard them as sacred animals, although the character of the habitat is in itself a powerful deterrent and may well ensure the survival of the Kiang herds.

The existence of the Kiang was first brought to the notice of natural scientists by another adventurer in the mould of Przewalski, discoverer of the Asiatic Wild Horse, and like him a player in the "great game" of Imperialist manoeuvring in central Asia. This one was an Englishman, William Moorcroft, a veterinary surgeon in the employment of the Bengal Army. He is acknowledged as the father of Himalayan exploration, although his exceptional achievements received little recognition in his lifetime, or even at his death in 1825. He was among the earliest explorers of Ladakh and Kashmir, and was the first Englishman to set foot on the banks of the Oxus on his epic journey to Bokhara. He died, it is said of fever, in his sixtieth year and is buried in an unmarked grave by that historic river.

TIBETAN KIANG These kiang inhabit the high plateau above the treeline. They are shy and difficult to approach, but perfectly adapted to the inhospitable environment.

IBERIAN
LEGACY

It is probable that the indigenous equine stock of the Iberian Peninsula was the first to be domesticated in Europe thousands of years ago and that it originated in Tarpan blood with an admixture of Asiatic Wild Horse. This early stock, crossed with North African Barbs, was to provide the genetic base for the Spanish, or Iberian, Horse, one of the most pervasive influences in equine development.

IBERIAN LEGACY

A hundred years ago, a period so short that it cannot be considered in the context of the long history of the horse and its development, there were wild horse herds in the Pyrenees, the mountain chain dividing France from Spain. The mountainous region of Asturia in Spain supported its own indigenous wild ponies, and there were others of very ancient origin in both Spain and Portugal. Today, the truly wild herds have gone but, though much decreased in numbers, there are still ponies kept in feral or semiferal conditions in these regions.

The first evidence of the black Ariègeois is in the carvings and wall pictures of Niaux made about 30,000 years ago.

PYRENEAN MOUNTAIN BREEDS

The three principal mountain breeds of the Pyrenees are the Landais, which ran in the wooded areas of the Landes region north of the border; the Basque Pottock, now divided into three types (standard; double, the largest of the three; and the pinto); and the Ariègeois, sometimes called *Cheval de Merens*, which is the mountain horse of Andorra and the high, eastern edges of the Pyrenean chain. The Landais, probably a close descendant of the wild Tarpan, was never much more than a semi-wild pony. It seems to have originated on the Barthes plains along the Adour River and is, indeed, sometimes known as the Barthais. It is now found on the Landais marshes around Dax. Efforts were made to improve the stock (which could have been in danger of becoming too much inbred) by the introduction of Arabian blood in 1900 and again in 1913, when there were about 2,000 ponies living on the marshy plain. Later, when the situation deteriorated still further, Welsh Riding Ponies were introduced to supplement the Arabian presence. Today, the Landais is entirely domesticated and is a useful riding pony of some quality.

▶ POTTOCK This is a pinto type of Basque Pottock, a tough, hardy breed that still lives in semiferal groups. These agile mountain ponies were used extensively by contraband smugglers.

A small part of the Basque Pottock population is still considered to be wild or at least semiferal. Its ground is in France's Basque region within the provinces of Labourd, Basse-Navarre and Soule. It is a mountain horse, tough, hardy, agile and surefooted, and well able to withstand extremes of climate. Both the Pottock and the bigger Ariègeois are used as pack animals, and both were employed extensively by smugglers to carry contraband over the mountain ridges right up to World War II, and probably after that. There are associations formed to conserve and improve the best elements of the Pottock herd and even a Stud Book which allows the use of Arabian and Welsh stallions on selected mares.

ASTURCON The mountainous
Asturia region of northern
Spain is home to the
Asturcon ponies, which
may have existed there
in isolated pockets before
the last ice age 10,000
years ago.

The old sort of Ariègeois, which takes its name from the Ariège river, was accurately described in the *Commentarii* of Julius Caesar (*Commentaries: notes on the Gallic and Cini Wars*). It is still to be found in a semiferal state in the fastnesses of the high *soulanes* around Andorra on the Spanish border. The first evidence of this black mountain pony is in the carvings and wall pictures at Niaux in the Ariège made about 30,000 years ago. It is depicted in full winter coat, dark and thick, and with a heavy mane and tail. Moreover the Cro-Magnon artist observed and included the characteristic "beard" growth covering the jawbones.

The habitat of the Ariègeois is very similar to that of the high Cumbrian fells in northern England. Solid black in color, the breed closely resembles the British Fell pony and is almost an exact replica of the heavier Dales pony.

The pony is so surefooted that it copes easily with the snow and ice that often covers the mountain trails. Protected by its thick coat the breed is impervious to cold, but it cannot tolerate heat and must seek shelter during the daytime in summer.

ASTURCON

The mountainous region of Asturia in the north of Spain was once, even up to 80 years ago, the inaccessible mountain habitat of large numbers of ponies living in wild herds. They were called Asturcon, and there is a very probable relationship between them and the Italian Bardigiano, whose habitat, in relative terms, is not that far away. It also resembles and has some of the character of the oldest of the British pony breeds, the Exmoor. It is not unreasonable to suppose that all three breeds have a common root in Celtic pony stock and that the Bardigiano and Asturcon represent isolated pockets of strains that existed before the last ice age (c. 10,000 BC) and have survived in their distinctive form up to the present time. The herds have now gone but a nucleus of Asturcon is conserved in a semiferal state.

Black in color, strong and very active, the Asturcon is now being used as a child's pony as a result of the formation some years ago of a Spanish Pony Club. The ponies, about 13.2hh. (137cm) in height, are particularly good jumpers.

Early Iberian stock was probably the first to be domesticated in Europe.

SORRAIA PONY

Even older than the Asturcon is Portugal's Sorraia pony, descending principally, it is thought, from the primitive Tarpan with an admixture of the Asiatic Wild Horse.

The Sorraia and its close relation over the river, the Portuguese Garrano, which also stems from the same primitive stock, were probably the first horses to be domesticated in Europe. If that is so, and no contrary evidence exists, it is these ponies crossed with the Barbs of North Africa that are responsible for the superlative Spanish Horse, whose prepotent blood was a major influence on the world's equine population well into the 18th century.

The indigenous Iberian stock, which for thousands of years was spread over the whole Peninsula, is now concentrated in particular areas. The Sorraia habitat lies in the plains between the Sor and Raia rivers (running

through both Portugal and Spain), while the Garrano or Minho, originally of the same root stock, is raised in the more fertile valleys of Garranos do Minho and Traz dos Montes in the north of Portugal.

SORRAIA The modern pony has been much improved and may sometimes resemble a miniature version of the Iberian Horse itself.

The Garrano, now much improved by the Portuguese Ministry of Agriculture, bears little resemblance to its primitive forebears. Continual infusions of Arabian blood have produced a refined pony of quality with a neat, pretty head right down to the concave Arabian profile.

This has not happened to the Sorraia, which, in many cases, reveals its primitive antecedents in conformation and coat color. Of course, improvements have been made by selective outcrossing, and the modern pony is very much more attractive than its predecessors. Some of them, indeed, are to all intents miniature versions—12–12.3hh. (120–130cm)—of the Iberian Horse itself, Lusitano, Andalucian, or Alter-Real, which again share a common root.

Fifty or sixty years ago the Sorraia was clearly a Tarpan derivative and even now the characteristics may persist. The upright shoulder is still evident, the straight back, large head and profile inclining to the convex, and there are the coat colors, too. The primitive mouse color is still to be seen together with the peculiar short, wiry, deerlike hair. Dun is a color that also occurs, as well as a dull, palomino yellow. They are usually accompanied by dorsal stripes and sometimes with the zebra markings round the lower limbs. The ears, too, are long, quite unlike the short, prick ears of the pony. They are set very high on the head and, as in the primitive horses, are tipped with black. It is exceptionally hardy and has the ability to survive in climatic extremes on minimal subsistence.

PORTUGESE HORSES The horses of present-day Portugal, principally the courageous Lusitano and the "classical" Alter-Real, epitomize all that is best about the beautiful and impressive Iberian Horse.

When agricultural mechanization was introduced the ponies became redundant for work on the land and the stock began to deteriorate. To preserve the Sorraia and the valuable gene bank it represented, the late Dr Ruy d'Andrade, a world authority associated with some of the most significant studies in equine development, kept a small, pure herd in the natural state, and the practice was continued after his death by his son Fernando. The herd was a principal factor in the conservation of the Sorraia, and though a wild herd no longer exists the animals are still kept in semiferal conditions.

Both the Mexican Galiceno, the smooth-gaited horse originating in Galicia, and the justly famous South American Criollo can claim a background of Sorraia blood; certainly the modern Galiceno is as close to original Sorraia type as can be found. It inherits the dun coloring and particularly the tough constitution, hard feet, and general adaptability of the primitive root.

GALICENO The Galiceno of Mexico has its origin in the famously smooth-gaited horses of Galicia and may trace its descent from Portugal's Sorraia breed.

◀ CRIOLLO, PATAGONIA This South American breed is among the toughest and most enduring in the world. Descending from early Spanish stock, influenced by the Barb, it also traces to Sorraia and Asturcon blood.

HORSES OF
THE STEPPES

Successive waves of horse-people had their origin in the steppelands of central Asia, from which nomadic warriors, mounted on their wiry ponies, established a pattern of armed migrations that began as early as the second millenium BC with the Kassites, Elamites, and Hyksos. Parthians and Scythians, the archetypal horse warriors, continued the expansion of the steppe dwellers, which culminated in the whirlwind of destruction created by Genghis Khan and his Mongols in the 13th century.

HORSES OF THE STEPPES

Asia is the world's largest continent, stretching from the Arctic Circle to the equator; and its steppelands, as yet largely unexploited, still provide a habitat for thousands and thousands of horses. The herds are no longer wild in the sense that the Tarpan and Asiatic Wild Horse were, but they live in feral conditions that have not changed since the last ice age and they are just as essential an element in the economy of the steppe people as they have ever been.

Central to the Asian horse breeds is the Mongolian pony, direct descendant of the Asiatic Wild Horse (*see* The Primitive Connection chapter 2. It is, in general, an unprepossessing animal, but it exerts a powerful and pervading influence throughout the continent. South of the Gobi Desert the ponies are not much over 12.1hh. (124cm) but a bigger type is bred in the western parts of Mongolia. They live on the steppe, surviving on minimal feed in some of the harshest climatic conditions in the world, and they are quite capable of traveling 50–60 mile (80–95kms) a day, while 150 miles (190km) is not uncommon. Racing is endemic to the Mongolian people, and races are held over distances that are often as great as 20–40 miles (30–65km). Nonetheless, the herds are also a source of meat and hides, the mares are milked, and dung provides fuel for fires.

The horses of the steppes live in feral conditions that have not changed since the last ice age.

Outer Mongolia has the largest number of horses per head of population in the world. It is this huge number of animals, combined with the inherited primitive vigor, obtained from a close relationship with the Asiatic Wild Horse, that is responsible for the widespread influence of the Mongolian blood, an influence that extends northwards almost to the Siberian uplands and west to the Urals and Kazakhstan. The ponies of the Altai carry Mongolian blood and so do the Kirghiz and the Kazakh.

Mongol stock may have had some effect upon the development of the Marwari horse of Rajasthan and the Kathiawari of Gujerat, although both are predominantly influenced by the Arabian and its derivatives of Asia Minor. There are close ties with the Tibetan pony (Nanfan), the Bhutia, and the Spiti and Zaskari on the Tibetan borders. Chinese ponies are clearly of Mongolian origin and so are those of Japan. The Mongolian influence continues with the Burma pony and the Manipuri of Assam and carries through to Indonesia.

▶ MONGOLIAN PONIES Huge numbers of Mongolian ponies still live on the steppelands and remain an essential element in the region's economy, providing for the needs of the nomadic herders.

Many steppe breeds are kept, as they have been for centuries, to produce meat, milk, and hides, and they support a sizeable industry in these commodities. Although production is well organized within the cooperative system the herds are kept in feral conditions the year round; it would be uneconomic and probably counterproductive to do otherwise.

KAZAKH AND KIRGHIZ

Notable steppe breeds are the Kazakh and Kirghiz horses and the Kazakh offshoots, the Dzhabe and Adaev types. Both Kazakh and Kirghiz stock are related to the Mongolian ponies and, to a degree, to the ancient Altai mountain strains. They have been crossed extensively and deliberately to develop animals suitable for meat production and dairy produce, and also to obtain improved working horses.

The Dzhabe and Adaev types, standing at about 14hh. (142cm), thrive on semidesert pasture and are hardy enough to endure the cold winters. Both have a high milk yield, and the Dzhabe provides good meat yield.

NANFAN PONIES These ponies do well on the summer pasture of the Tibetan plateau and are well able to cope with the far harsher winter conditions.

MONGOLIAN HORSE Sheep and horses, both essential to the nomad economy, share the extensive grazing of the Mongolian steppes, being moved on from one pasturage to the next.

For the most part the horses are coarse in appearance although outcrossing has given greater refinement to the Adaev. Indeed, the Adaev is claimed to be an excellent riding horse and very fast over long distances. However, while the Adaev does well enough on the semidesert pasturage of southern Kazakhstan, it has lost the inbred ability of the Dzhabe to endure the fiercely cold winters in the north. It is, perhaps, a prime example of the effects of primitive dilution by "improving" influences.

BURYAT

While attempts may have been made to improve the Buryat, one of the smallest of the Siberian ponies, it contrives to remain much closer to the primitive root through the influence of the Mongolian pony. The ponies

are distinguished by a massive body carried on short, powerful legs, which are frequently zebra-marked, and long, thick hair with which the body is covered. The protection of an exceptionally thick impenetrable coat is, indeed, a necessity in view of the below-freezing temperatures that are typical of their habitat. It goes without saying that these are extraordinarily hardy animals, possessed of the strongest constitution.

The Buryat is an important source of milk, meat and hides, while the thick coat hair is woven to make felt and clothing, a practice commonplace among nomadic horse-people from time immemorial. This remarkable little horse is also versatile enough to be used under saddle and in harness and, despite the necessarily short action imposed by the conformation, it is reputed to be fast and enduring.

BASHKIR

Probably the best known of the steppe breeds is the Bashkir, largely because of the American interest in the Bashkir "Curly," which has resulted in the formation of an American Bashkir Curly Register, as well as "breed" associations supported by some very dubious theorizing. In the context of a wild or semiferal horse study, the antecedents of the American Bashkir are not of consequence. In the country of its origin, the Bashkir, or Bashkirsky, without the appendage Curly, is adequately documented.

The breed evolved in the southern foothills of the Urals where it would have been subject to a variety of influences over a long period of time, including, in more recent times, outcrossing to Russian riding horses as well as to harness horses. As a result, two types have emerged, the steppe Bashkir and the slightly smaller mountain horse. In fact, both average about 14hh. (142cm). The herds are kept in their natural habitat the year round and are capable of surviving winter temperatures of 22–40°F (30–40°C) below freezing, as well as the fierce blizzards bringing snow that may lie as deep as 3ft (70cm) and more.

The Bashkir is notably wide-bodied with a massive head and short, fleshy neck. The back is broad and straight, the croup rounded and sloping, and the withers are flat and round. The whole is carried on short, strong legs. The coat, like that of the Buryat, is thick and impenetrable by wind, or wet, and the combings are used similarly in the making of felt and clothing. When compared to horses that are not adapted to life on the steppes, it is an unusual and very special coat, *but it is not curly*. American sources claim that the hair of the Bashkir does not cause any reaction in people allergic to horses. However, there is no mention of this in the official description of the Bashkir and, in any event, one imagines that allergic reactions to horses would be rare among the horse-people of central Asia.

In the breed's traditional homeland of the Bashkirian steppes it was officially recognized as being integral to the local economy some 160 years ago. Breeding centers were established in 1845 although the animals were still kept under natural conditions. The employment of selective breeding methods increased the effective use of the Bashkir in agriculture, transport, and so on, but the primary purpose was to improve productivity in respect of meat and dairy products. To support this end, a development programme was instituted to build processing plants and creameries, and to improve the transport system.

Bashkir mares, their natural diet supplemented in very severe weather by a ration of steppe-grown hay, have a surprisingly high milk yield. During a seven to eight-month lactation period the average yield is in the region of

330 gallons (1,500 liters), while the best milkers will produce as much as 550 gallons (2,700 litres).The Bashkirs are also enduring horses under saddle, while in harness it is said that a pair will pull a sleigh for some 75–85 miles (20–140km) in the space of 24 hours, and that without any supplementary feed. In fact, of course, every breed raised in the steppe environment is well able to fulfil a wide variety of purposes—as they have done for thousands of years. Human intervention has only improved and extended an inbuilt versatility.

It is claimed that the American Bashkir Curly is "one of the greatest mysteries of the American horse world" when, in fact, it may be no more than a case of mistaken identity and unsubstantiated assumption. Without any doubt, the theory postulating the arrival of the Bashkir, along with its owners, over the landbridges of the Bering Strait (prior to its disappearance at the end of the ice age), is untenable, and, moreover, displays a flagrant disregard for, or perhaps ignorance of, proven historical fact. Horses and humans may well have entered America by that route, but the horse became extinct on the American continent 8,000 or more years ago, and it is absolutely certain that the horses brought to the Americas by the Spanish *conquistadores* of the 16th century had not the remotest connection with those of the Bashkirian steppes.

> **That the steppe herds can thrive in their inhospitable environment derives directly from the primitive vigor of their origin.**

It is now suggested that the Lokai of Southern Tadzhistan, on the borders of Afghanistan and a very, very long way from even the most southern extremities of the Urals, could be the originator of the Bashkir "Curly." There is no possibility of that, nor is there any evidence of a Lokai influence in the Bashkir, but it could be that the three curly-coated horses seen by Peter Damele near Austin, Nevada, in 1898, were of a Lokai strain. Thick, curly hair, on the authority of the Russian Ministry of Agriculture, does occur occasionally in some chestnut-colored Lokai horses, although the characteristic coat is not necessarily passed on with 100 percent consistency.

It is possible that the occasional importation of horses to Alaska from Russia in the early 19th century might have included Lokai stock, and perhaps others, although it is suggested that the bulk would have been of Yakut origin since that breed existed in the region of Okhotsk, the port for the ships bound for Alaska. However, there is no evidence to support the assumption. So perhaps there is an element of mystery. What is indisputable is that the American Bashkir has no connection with the Bashkir of the Urals.

A MILLION
MUSTANGS

Will James, the archetypal Westerner, wrote that the Mustangs of the American West belonged "not to man but to that country of junipers and sage, of deep arroyas, mesas — and freedom." A romantic view, but it did not prevent thousands being canned for pet food. In the end, the weight of public opinion halted the slaughter and today's Mustangs are protected by law and handfuls of welfare associations.

A MILLION MUSTANGS

At the beginning of the 20th century a million or more wild—or, more accurately, *feral*—horses inhabited the western states of America. That number is possibly now reduced to about 30,000. Increasingly the present-day herds are protected by law and by the activities of numerous welfare and conservation societies that reflect public concern for a heritage that is as integral to the American West as any. The impact of the feral herds on the American culture is evident in the number of place names derived from their presence all over the western plains. The state of Texas, for example, has 27 Mustang Creeks, almost as many Horse Hollows, a town called Wild Horse, and the Wild Horse Desert.

Viewed objectively, the Mustang represents a unique genetic heritage well worth preserving.

Mustang, like so much American horse vocabulary, is derived from the Spanish, in this instance the word *mesteño*, which means a group or herd of horses. These were horses that had escaped or strayed from their supervised range and had reverted to the wild state, in time acquiring the survival skills necessary for the feral life. They were not, of course, truly wild horses and, indeed, are now recognized by the Bureau of Land Management as "the American feral horse." (The only surviving truly *wild* horse (as opposed to ass or zebra) in the world is Przewalski's, *see* The Primitive Connection, chapter 2).

The Mustang herds originated with the cattle-ranching settlements established by the early Spanish settlers in the American southwest. By the opening years of the 17th century these ranching enterprises had bred and acquired large numbers of horses. In the open conditions of the cattle ranges some of this stock became feral and as early as 1579 herds of such horses were spreading northwards in large numbers from central Mexico. Originally, these were Spanish horses, or their descendants, many of them showing the character of their Barb antecedent. They would usually have been about 14hh.(142cm) in height and there would have been a variety of coat colors.

▶ MUSTANGS In some areas there has been an inevitable degeneration in the Mustang stock, but otherwise there are many quality animals to be found.

Later these herds were joined by feral horses from the eastern states, pushed westward by the incursions of the early colonists. French blood in horses of Norman and Norman-Breton stock introduced a new mix to the western herds; and there was also the influence of the old-type East Friesian, product of a genetic melting pot of half-a-dozen European coach breeds but with Oldenburg as the predominant ingredient.

At the turn of the 19th century the US government was importing these heavy, warmblood coach horses to pull artillery pieces and for use in general military transport. In the course of constant skirmishing and the minor battles fought by the US cavalry in the west, some of these horses would have joined the feral herds to give a new element to the Mustang population.

It was the acquisition of Mustangs that altered life for the Native Americans of the Great Plains and made them the last to become one of the world's horse-people. These horses were, too, just as essential to the growth of the American West. Mustangs were caught up in a variety of ways by professional "bronco busters" to be broken in rough and ready fashion for the cowboys working the huge cattle herds. Bronco (or *broncho*) again comes from the Spanish and means wild or unruly; in the north bronco was often the name given to the Mustang.

MUSTANG MARES AND FOALS

This is an exemplary group of Mustangs in which the foals are well grown and possessed of notably good limbs, while the adults are good, quality specimens.

DEPLETION AND CONSERVATION

The Mustang population increased up to the turn of the 20th century when their numbers were fast becoming an environmental problem: they denied grazing to domestic stock, and many were shot by ranchers and stockmen. In the 1930s as many as 100,000 Mustangs were being killed in a year, and by the 1970s organized killing on a large scale had seriously depleted the herds, active encouragement being given by the demands of the meat market created largely by petfood manufacturers.

MUSTANG HERD Mustang herds, protected by law, are found in America's western states. Their numbers are regulated and the natural range is carefully preserved.

At this point it is probable that the herds amounted to no more than 17,000–18,000 head spread over the nine western states. The government took action by recognizing the Mustang in law as an endangered species and designating wild horse refuges in less accessible areas of the country, particularly in Wyoming and Montana. Importantly, the public conscience was also aroused. Today the welfare groups that were formed subsequently are active in legislative activities to protect the animals and, necessarily, to preserve the natural range. Others are concerned with research programs, and some concentrate on providing practical help in the field by maintaining water supplies and providing essential minerals, such as salt.

The first Mustang support group was the Spanish Mustang Registry. It was not a conventional welfare society. It was founded by a Wyoming Mustang breeder, Robert Brislawn, in 1957 with the object of perpetuating the old Spanish strains of both Barb and Andalucian type whose ancestors had gone feral 400 years before. "We're trying to restore a breed, not create one," said Brislawn, and he operated the registry on the strictest procedural lines, refusing to enter horses that showed evidence of outcrossing and that did not come within the laid-down guidelines in respect of character and appearance.

In the 1970s, the Mustang was officially recognized as an endangered animal.

The American Mustang Association was formed in the 1960s, and it was followed in 1972 by the Spanish Barb Breeders' Association. The former sought to preserve and promote the American Mustang "...through registration and an intelligent breeding program." The latter was concerned with restoration of the "true Spanish Barb horse" based on documented descriptions made between the 15th and 18th centuries. It formulated a breed standard on the basis of its research and encouraged highly selective breeding practices.

A PREPOTENT INFLUENCE

Whether or not a breed has been "restored" or "created" is not of much consequence. The various societies have been able to safeguard strains, or related strains, that are no longer to be found in the Old World and now survive in the environments that have been instrumental in fixing their original character.

There can be no overall, definitive description of the Mustang, if only because of the number of different breeds and types involved in so vast an area; but without doubt, the Spanish influence is distinctive and that says much for the prepotency of the Spanish and Barb horses. Certainly, Robert Brislawn was quite clear about the type of horse he wanted in Wyoming. His ideal was a fairly small, compact horse of about 14hh. (142cm) and weighing about 800lb (360kg). It was to be shortbacked, low in the withers, and with a low, sloping croup.

After studying skeletal remains, Brislawn believed that the horse, which he termed primitive Barb ("primitive" meaning early in the context of the American horse population following the Spanish conquests) should have 17 ribs and 5 lumbar vertebrae like the Arabian horse, rather than the 18 ribs and 6 lumbar vertebrae of other breeds, which seems to contradict the requirements for a sloping croup. Many authorities might have difficulty in equating Brislawn's contention with the reality of the modern Spanish Barb types, few of which appear to have that conformational structure. He was on less controversial ground when defining the coat coloration, which ranges from roan or *grulla* (slate-blue to mouse-brown), to dun and buckskin (dark cream). Mane, tail, and lower limbs are black, the head is neat, and the small ears are rimmed with black hair.

MUSTANG ADOPTION SCHEME

While the Mustang support groups seek to conserve and manage the horses within the parameters set by the "ecological balance" of the range, there is also an Adopt-a-Horse program, which was begun in 1973 in the Pryor Mountains of Montana. In an effort to assist the humane redistribution of excess animals, it allows members of the public to buy a Mustang for a nominal sum. After a probationary period, to ensure that the animal can be kept properly, the horse becomes the outright property of the adopter.

With experienced and skilful horse-people the adopted feral horse may become a cooperative and pleasurable animal to ride and drive, but for the less knowledgeable it could as easily become a problem horse, and this has to be a consideration. Whether the scheme contributes materially in reducing the number of excess animals might be thought a matter for conjecture.

◀ MUSTANG STALLIONS
Mustang stallions will fight for control of their mare group during the breeding season, but usually without either contestant being seriously injured.

A PLAGUE
OF BRUMBIES

The principal habitat of the Australian Brumby herds is mainly to the west of Brisbane, Queensland. Descended from horses that strayed from the mining settlements created during the Australian Gold Rush of 1851, numbers had increased so greatly by the 1960s that the Brumby had become a serious problem. The resulting slaughter of thousands of horses, often conducted from helicopters, provoked worldwide condemnation.

A PLAGUE OF BRUMBIES

Without doubt the American Mustang has fared incomparably better than its feral equivalent in Australia, the Brumby, which attracts little or no conservationist support.

The Brumby is a remarkably self-reliant and inherently tough animal.

The first horses to be imported into Australia came from the Cape of Good Hope and were landed in Sydney Cove on January 26, 1788. They included a significant percentage of Arabians and Thoroughbreds, and it was from this group and later imports that the modern Australian Stock Horse evolved. Within 40 years of the first importation, the forerunner of the Stock Horse—the Australian Waler—was established in the colony of New South Wales, from which it took its name. It has been described as "probably the best saddle horse in the world." R. S. Summerhays, the noted authority responsible for that statement, had himself been a remount officer and his remark was made in the context of a cavalry remount.

In World War I, the Waler consolidated its already enviable reputation when Australia provided over 120,000 horses for the Allied armies. Many of them served in Allenby's classic cavalry campaign in which the Desert Mounted Corps defeated the Turkish army in Palestine during 1917–18. Indian cavalry up to World War II were mounted on Walers, which the civilian administration preferred over the Indian countrybred. At home, in Australia, the Waler was the all-round versatile horse of the huge sheep stations and absolutely invaluable to the industry. Between 15hh. (152cm) and 16hh. (163cm), it was enduring, hardy, and able to tolerate high temperatures. It was not fast, but it was enormously agile and seldom sick or sorry.

▶ BRUMBY The Brumby, by nature a wild animal, is wary, cunning and, on its own ground, very difficult to approach and even more difficult to catch.

The Brumby was descended from just such horses. In the years following the Australian Gold Rush of 1851 many horses strayed from the early mining settlements to run loose in the rough scrub country. There they multiplied over and over again until within the space of a hundred years they had become a serious nuisance. They were looked upon as vermin by stockmen anxious to protect the grazing of their domestic stock from the depredations of the destructive feral horses, and the stockmen destroyed them by every available means. But, as with the American Mustang, it was the pet-food industry that encouraged the specific hunting of Brumbies. In fact the shooting of feral horses became an acceptable weekend sport for many Australians.

By the 1960s the wholesale slaughter of the Brumbies had escalated to such a degree that it provoked worldwide condemnation and caused the Australian authorities great, and not wholly undeserved, embarrassment. Using jeeps, light aircraft and helicopters, trigger-happy hunters were pursuing and shooting thousands of horses. In one area, 700 miles (1,100km) west of Brisbane, 8,000 horses were shot; some, inevitably, were wounded rather than killed and were left to die in the bush. Similar numbers were exterminated elsewhere, 9,000 on one property alone. It was a brutal business, and even now it is not forgotten.

There is no doubt that the Brumbies had deteriorated physically as a result of living in an environment that was unable to sustain such numbers, but they had also developed uncanny instincts of survival, frequently evading pursuit, and acquiring much native cunning. Moreover, the Brumby is remarkably self-reliant and as inherently tough as its predecessors.

The best specimens might make useful saddle horses, although the Brumby is reputed to be wild by nature and in consequence difficult to tame. In any event Australians have plenty of good-quality domestic horses, and it would hardly be sensible to spend time catching and schooling second-rate animals of minimal potential. In short the Brumby is not needed, and its destructive presence is not appreciated.

It would be unacceptable from every viewpoint to attempt to eliminate the wild horse population. The only alternative has to be the intelligent management of the Brumby herds, and that involves the implementation and public acceptance of a humane culling policy to control their numbers and contain what has become a real problem.

◀ BRUMBY GRAZING While grazing by small groups of horses does not present a difficulty to stockmen, large herds can be damaging to the interests of domestic animals.

SEA AND
ISLAND

First among the horses of sea and island is the Camargue, an ancient breed indigenous
to the marshlands of the Rhône. But, surprisingly in the 21st century, there are horse
herds still living in island habitats. Horses have inhabited Sable Island, off the coast
of Nova Scotia, for over 250 years. Ponies have been on Chincoteague and Assateague,
off the American coast, since colonial days. More recently, since 1928, ponies have lived
on Lundy Island in Britain's Bristol Channel.

SEA AND ISLAND

The combination of horses and sea has been the source of romantic inspiration ever since Poseidon of the white horses was declared God of the Sea, "the embodiment of all horses, their God and Lord." Poets eulogize on the beauty of silky white coats and flowing manes the color of sea foam, and often the inspiration for their verse is the Camargue Horse.

Sea, salt, people, horses, and bulls make up the Camargue's elemental character.

HORSES OF THE CAMARGUE

An early admirer, George Meredith (1828–1909), wrote:
"...Still with white form fleck'd are they,
And when the sea puffs black from grey,
And ships part cables, loudly neigh
The stallions of Camargue, all joyful in the roar."

Well, it is not quite like that but, allowing for poetic licence, the Camargue horse is certainly a striking animal, effortlessly complementing the harsh, inhospitable wildness of the environment of which it is a product. The homeland of the Camargue lies between the Mediterranean sea, the River Rhône, and the old town of Aigne-Mortes in the south of France. In summer the hot, fierce sun bakes the ground until it cracks. In winter nature covers this hard place with a winding sheet of salt water. The all-pervading salt is brought by the tearing *mistral*, the wind that bends the stunted shrub growth to the ground and dries to the consistency of parched leather the faces of the men and women who, nonetheless, take a fierce pride in this swampland of the Rhône delta to which they were born. They call it "the most noble conquered territory of man," and it satisfies their independent character to know that it is not easily subdued. The people, together with the wind, the salt, the sea, the horses, and the fierce, black fighting bulls, make up the elemental character of the place.

▶ HORSES OF THE SEA These striking white horses, flecked with spume as though rising out of the sea, encapsulate the very spirit of this fierce swampland of the Camargue.

The free life in the *manades* (herds) has endowed the Camargue horses with a special character, including exceptional hardiness. But, when examined objectively, the legendary white horses are not all that beautiful and even the coat—the declared crowning glory of the Camargue—is rough when examined at close quarters. The heads are coarse and heavy, the necks are short, and the shoulders are upright. The overall impression is of a primitive ancestry with overtones of the North African Barb.

In compensation, there are long, thick and photogenic manes and tails and, more to the point, there is a great depth of girth, good back and, though the croup slopes sharply, the short structure is one of great strength. The limbs, too, are well formed, and the feet, though large to conform with the marsh environment, are hard and sound—so hard, in fact, that the Camargue horses are rarely shod. The horses' hardiness is essential in conditions of extreme climatic change limiting the growth of sustainable feed. They live on what can be scavenged from the saltladen marshland: tough grasses, reeds, and saltwort shared with the black cattle, which, like the horse, are the pride of the Camargue.

The Camargue is a small horse, about 14hh. (142cm) or even smaller. It matures slowly, and is not fully developed until it is between five and seven years old, but it is longlived and often leads an active life after the age of 25. In direct contrast to the all-black cattle, the coat of the Camargue is white and is its greatest visual asset. The foals are not born white, but are either iron-gray, black, or a mottled brown, turning to white as they get older.

A peculiarity of the Camargue is the distinctive action. The walk is long, and exceptionally active, but the trot, on account of those straight shoulders, is short and stilted and would be very uncomfortable to ride. For that reason the trot is seldom if ever employed, the *gardian*—keeper of the Camargue and the Gallic version of the American cowboy—preferring to ride in walk or, more usually, in canter and gallop, both of which paces are surprisingly free.

HARSH ENVIRONMENT The hardy white horses of the Camargue are well able to live on the reeds, tough grasses and saltwort provided by their marsh environment.

CAMARGUE A picture evocative of the romance of the Camargue, to which the white horses are as integral as the sea and the mistral.

Although the landscape of the Rhône evolves to accord with modern pressures—such as tourism and a rice-growing project on upwards of 40,000 acres—the traditional work of the *gardians* is the raising of the fierce and fast black bulls for the bullring. In this it is the Camargue horse that is the vital link between man and bull. It is bred to the bull; and if its feet are large it is, nonetheless, quick on them and inherently surefooted. It works the bulls like a sheepdog works a flock, and it does so without fear, displaying a courage that is remarkable in a species whose instinctive defence mechanism is based on swift unreasoning flight.

The early origins of the breed are impossible to state definitively, but the informed consensus believes the Camargue to have been indigenous to the area from prehistory. Largely owing to the efforts of one enthusiast, Etienne Saurel, a notable hippologist, the Camargue was recognized as a breed by the National Stud Services in 1968. Had it not been for the independence of the breeders, recognition would most probably have been given long before, but an association was formed, if reluctantly, and annual stallion inspections are organized under the aegis of the Nimes National Stud. The region sustains some 30 *manades* with a complement of about 40-odd stallions (*grignons*) and 400 broodmares.

While there can be no certainty, the animals depicted in the cave drawings at Lascaux and Niaux, dated *c.*15,000 BC, bear a strong resemblance to the Camargue. It is also suggested that prehistoric horse remains found in the 19th century at Solutre, in the Charollais country of France, might be those of the earliest Camargues, the bones appearing to be proportionate to those of the modern horse. The find at Solutre is dated as being as much as 50,000 years old.

The horses and the bulls of the Carmargue remain a central element in the lives of the people.

In later times an obvious influence was that of the Asian and Mongol horses that passed through this country with the Ostro-Goths and Vandals of the pre-Christian era. A millennium or so after that, in the 7th and 8th centuries, the predominating impact of the North African Barb reached the Camargue lands with the Moorish conquerors of the Iberian Peninsula. That powerful blood still persists today in the modern Camargue horse, while the association is made even more evident in the saddlery and horselore of the *gardian*. The saddle, down to the cage-type stirrups, is unmistakably Iberian, developed on the Peninsula during the long Moorish occupation. The *gardian* rides longlegged, like the South American *gaucho* or the Californian cowboy, and he uses a lariat, too, when catching up animals in the corrals. To handle the cattle he has a long, forked pole, the *pique*, similar to that employed in Iberia for the same purpose.

Today, much of the Camargue is under cultivation but the horses and the bulls remain a central element in the lives of the people. The horses still work the cattle and drive the bulls at full speed through the streets of Sainte Marie de la Mer and elsewhere during the colorful traditional folk festivals. It is a practice to set the adrenalin racing, and it is undoubtedly dangerous, but it makes for a wonderful tourist attraction.

A huge nature reserve of 17,000 acres (7,000 hectares) has been created around the lagoon of Etang de Vaccarès. This popular tourist attraction creates a new use for the horses of the Camargue, for there is no better way to see the wildlife than from the back of a horse.

SABLE ISLAND

Horses living on islands evoke thoughts of ships wrecked on treacherous coasts and, indeed, there are tales aplenty of shipwrecked horses, most, if not all, being wholly unsubstantiated. Connemaras, New Forest ponies, Dartmoors and Exmoors, as well as the Kathiawari of the Indian subcontinent and a handful of Indonesian ponies, are supposedly influenced by horses that swam to the shore from wrecked vessels. There is a similar story to explain, in part, the presence of horses on Sable Island, which lies some 100 miles (160km) off the east coast of Nova Scotia, and like the others there is no reason to think of it as other than a convenient fairytale.

Sable Island, known also as "the Dark Island" and "the Graveyard of the Atlantic," is a very unlikely place to find wild, or feral, horses. It is little more than a narrow, desolate sandbank, 30 miles (48km) long and just 1 mile (1.6km) wide, and the approaches to the island are hazardous. Vegetation consists of low shrub growth, the coarse grasses of the sand dunes, and the wild pea plants that grow along the water's edge. There are no trees to afford shelter against the Atlantic storms, and it is often covered in sea fogs. Altogether it is an inhospitable place.

Remarkably, the island has been inhabited and has supported domestic animals since the 16th century, when Portuguese expeditions to Canada put cattle and pigs on the island and gave it the name Santa Cruz. However, there is no evidence of any horses being put ashore or being seen there. The tentative Portuguese expeditions were followed by more determined French colonists, and in 1627 the Company of New France was formed. Isaac de Razilly was appointed Lieutenant-General of New France (called Canada) and Governor of Acadia (which later, under British rule, was renamed New Scotland—Nova Scotia).

▶ SABLE ISLAND PONIES

The horses of Sable Island are not so striking or as well known as those of the Camargue, but their story is not without an element of romance.

Razilly's small fleet of three ships landed there in 1632 carrying prospective settlers, seeds, tools, livestock, and horses of Norman or Norman-Breton stock. Even then these would have been influenced, if only in small measure, by the Norfolk Roadster, of which there is evidence in so many of the great French breeds, and they would have certainly carried a percentage of Arabian and Barb blood, introduced to upgrade the heavier Norman mares. None of the first complement of horses is recorded as having been put on Sable Island, although the island was then supporting 800 cattle, which were kept for the provision of meat and hides.

Another hundred years was to pass before the presence of horses on Sable Island was confirmed. The first mention of them was made in 1738, and it is from this date that it is possible to trace the fortunes of the Sable Island herd. Andrew Le Mercier, a Huguenot minister from Boston, rented the island in that year and, 15 years later, when he was disposing of his holdings, he wrote: "When I took possession of the Island, there were no four-footed creatures upon it but a few foxes, some red and some black; now there are I suppose about 90 sheep, between 20 and 30 horses, including colts, stallions, and breeding mares, about 30–40 cows, tame and wild, and 40 hogs."

By this time the original Acadian horses had been joined by imports of English horses, early "Thoroughbreds" and Roadsters, and by Spanish-based stock descended from the horses brought to America by the *conquistadores*. It was from this amalgam of bloods that the Sable Island herd derived. Several small herds, or groups, had been established by 1801, when James Morris, the first to hold the appointment, was the superintendent of the island. Morris estimated that there were about 90 horses there at that time. He described them as "wild" and being "of a middling size ... three quarters of them bay and the rest various colored." He wrote that they were, "very fleet and have in general a very handsome trot and canter." With difficulty, Morris was able to capture some of them and break them to saddle. He found them extraordinarily surefooted, very fast, and able to go over rough ground all day.

In 1885 another observer stated that: "The horses trot, jump, gallop, paddle, rack, prance, shuffle and waltz"— accomplishments that might be thought more suited to the circus big top than an Atlantic sandbank. The same observer remarked on the speed and hardiness of the horses, and on their ability to jump gulches (ravines) 4.5m (15ft) wide and more when being ridden to round up the wild stock.

"The horses trot, jump, gallop, paddle, rack, prance, shuffle and waltz."

Between 1884 and 1911, Robert J. Boutilier, the most successful of the island's administrators, carried out extensive land improvements, planting tussock grass, clovers and so on, as well as thousands of saplings and shrubs. Stallions, as well as some mares, were imported at the same time and put out with the Sable herds. There were some Thoroughbreds, a Morgan cross, a Standardbred trotter, Hackneys of the Roadster stamp and the then popular Thoroughbred/Clydesdale cross. Two Belgian Draught horses were also introduced in an unsuccessful effort to increase weight and size. Not all could survive the ferocious attacks of the intensely territorial Sable stallions, and even more were unable to withstand the climate, the terrain, and the paucity of forage. Those that could adapt, however, proved their worth by increasing the numbers and quality of the herds to the point where stock could be sent for sale to the mainland and even to the faraway West Indies.

Today the island supports some 200–300 head, split into small herds that keep pretty much to their own territories. Studies made in the late 1970s by Dr D. A. Welsh, of Dalhousie University, described the horses as being about 14hh. (142cm) and resembling the Barb of North Africa in appearance. Other descriptions criticize the heavy heads and drooping quarters, but these features are also characteristic of the Barb, which is recognized as one of the toughest horses in the world and—a point to note—one of the most prepotent, for it is the Barb character that has persisted in the Sable Island stock. The versatility, speed, courage, strength, and stamina of the Sable Island horse has not, at any time, been disputed.

The Sable Island horse represents a valuable gene bank.

Daniel Welsh concluded that "...the unique characteristics of these horses as a whole are undoubtedly due to exposure to the rigors of the environment over many generations without human interference." For that reason the Sable Island horse represents a valuable gene bank, worth preserving for its ability to reinvigorate more artificially created types and breeds.

CHINCOTEAGUE

About 700 miles (1,100km) to the south of Nova Scotia there are island horses whose origins are less documented than those of Sable Island, although they, too, have the obligatory shipwreck story. These largely nondescript feral ponies, which often have the character of stunted horses, have an average height of not much over 12hh. (122cm). They are to be found on the islands of Chincoteague (euphemistically translated as Beautiful Land across the Waters), from which they take their name, and Assateague; these islands lie off the coast of Maryland and Virginia.

The ponies, which at one time would have been regarded as scrub stock, cannot compare with the high-couraged Camargue or the vigorous Sable Island horses. The Chincoteague has, however, suffered from degeneration for significant periods in its history and, while its management has been well-meaning it has been fragmented by groups with perhaps conflicting interests and has not always, as a result, been of the highest order. Even today the scenario is confused and it is difficult to trace a progressive development.

Twenty years ago it was accepted that the 200-odd ponies lived on the 9,000-acre (3,600-hectare), 37-mile (60-km) long island of Assateague, which then as now was a national park. Until the exceptional storms of 1933 the island was connected to the mainland. It was that causeway, it may be presumed, which allowed stray or abandoned horses of the early American colonial days to make their home there.

Management has been well meaning but not always of the highest order.

Both Chincoteague and Assateague were the property of the Chincoteague Volunteer Fire Department, which from the 1920s, took responsibility for the ponies' welfare. Then in 1943 came the Federal Fish and Wildlife Service, a government conservation agency with a remit to encourage the varied wildfowl and seabird population of Assateague. The objective was commendable enough but not entirely compatible with the interests of the ponies. In an illjudged effort to preserve the wildfowl habitat the FFWS fenced off its "government-built pools." As a result the ponies were confined to a small, low-lying and marshy part of the island and their available grazing was reduced substantially. Moreover, it denied the ponies access to the sea, where they went in summer to avoid the hordes of biting mosquitoes. It was because of these enclosures that many ponies were trapped by the unusually high storm tides of 1962 and were drowned.

Public opinion and awareness had, indeed, already been aroused by the publication of Marguerite Henry's book *Misty of Chincoteague*, written in 1947, and then by the subsequent 20th Century Fox film *Misty*. Not great literature or great movie-making, but both improved the lot and standing of the Chincoteague ponies even while presenting them through rose=tinted spectacles. Today, the less acceptable history is conveniently forgotten and the National Park Service and the National Chincoteague Pony Association put out their own version, supported, it has to be hoped, by improved standards of management.

▶ CHINCOTEAGUE Evidence of the introduction of Pinto crosses, which share a common early root, is very apparent in the Chincoteague coat colors and in the usually common heads.

The ponies are now split into two herds, one at the Virginia end of Assateague and one at the Maryland end. The two are divided by a fence at the Virginia–Maryland state line, and each herd, split up into small family groups, is restricted to about 150 animals in the interests of the general ecology. The National Park Service owns and manages the Maryland herd while the Chincoteague Volunteer Fire Company owns and manages the Virginia herd. The last named is allowed grazing on the Chincoteague National Wildlife Refuge, by courtesy of a special use permit issued by none other than the Fish and Wildlife Service! This herd, too, is restricted to 150 animals and is known as the Chincoteague pony herd.

It is the Virginia end of this complex enterprise that is responsible for the event that attracts the attention of commentators and the public. Without the "Pony Penning," held since 1924 on the last Wednesday and Thursday of July, in aid of the Fire Company, the ponies might lapse into obscurity and further degeneration. On the Wednesday the herd is rounded up and, with the encouragement of the "saltwater cowboys" and cheered on by the assembled crowds, persuaded to swim across the channel to Chincoteague. The foals are auctioned off on Thursday and the rest of the herd swims back to Assateague. The Virginia herd it is claimed, with some correctness, is regularly inspected, vaccinated, and dewormed, and has its feet trimmed. It is also fenced off from the road to prevent animals from being injured.

The National Park Service's Maryland herd, which has grown in recent years in excess of the permitted 120–150 animals, is now subjected to an exercise in birth control as part of a "longterm horse population management program." The increasing number of animals was causing overgrazing and having a detrimental effect upon the dune and marsh habitat. To preserve the ecological balance the authorities developed a unique contraceptive vaccine capable of being delivered by dart gun.

In stock of this background there is no fixity of type. The animals lack substance and bone to some degree, and are often structurally weak, so they can hardly be regarded as a valued gene bank, but they have adapted to and survived in one of the least horse-friendly environments imaginable. Eighty percent of the feed intake on the island is composed of saltmarsh cordgrass and American beachgrass, supplemented by twigs, stems, seaweeds, and ivy. The diet lacks essential minerals with the exception of salt, and there is too much of that. The high salt concentration causes the animals to drink a correspondingly large quantity of water, far more than the usual intake of the domestic horse. Not surprisingly, it causes them to have a bloated appearance.

> The isolated environment of an island can help to encourage special qualities in feral or semiferal animals.

Efforts were made in the past to introduce outside blood to reinvigorate stock that had obvious constitutional strength if little else. Welsh ponies were used and probably some Shetlands, but the greatest influence was the Pinto, the legacy of which is very apparent in the herds. The choice of the Pinto was logical enough since the Pinto and the Chincoteague share a common root in the early Spanish stock. Otherwise, the Pinto is responsible for the not very attractive heads, which are a noticeable feature of the Chincoteague herds. No mention is made of similar efforts to upgrade the stock in recent years.

There is a market for the stock for use as children's ponies but demand is not significant. In general, and in view of the less than satisfactory end product, the efficacy of so complex a system of management is open to question.

LUNDY

An island environment, where the stock is isolated from outside influences, can help to encourage special qualities in feral or semiferal animals if it is properly managed. Sable Island is an example and so, too, is the much smaller Lundy Pony enterprise on Lundy Island in the Bristol Channel.

Lundy is described as a lump of granite, 3½ miles (5.5km) long by ½ mile (800m) wide, rising out of the sea where Britain's Bristol Channel meets the Atlantic. Lying north to south it is exposed to the strong southwesterly gales on the west; the east side is more sheltered, if not by very much. Despite the hard climatic conditions, it is rich in flora and fauna and, since 1928, has supported a small pony herd.

New Forest ponies—hardy, inherently sound and independent—were put on the island in 1928 by Lundy's owner Martin Coles Harman. By judicious use of outside stallions his object was to create a sort of super British native pony of distinctive character and appearance while retaining, in even greater measure than before, the hardiness, surefooted free movement, courage, and inborn sagacity of the native breeds. The sea-trip for the pioneer group was not made without difficulty, and the ponies had to swim from the boat to the shore. One of the stallions was a Thoroughbred, and he and his stock, not surprisingly, did not thrive in the hard winter conditions of Lundy. Later introductions of Welsh and particularly Connemara stock were much more successful, and the Connemara in particular is responsible for the distinctive Lundy type.

The pony averages 13hh. (132cm) in height. It is strongly built and deep-girthed, with an excellent, sloped riding shoulder. The limbs are as good as any to be found and the neat, knowing pony head is exceptionally attractive. The ponies, like the Connemara forebears, are good natural jumpers both in the show ring and cross country. In short, the conformation and performance is of the highest standard. The Connemara/Thoroughbred cross is reckoned to produce the very best sort of event horse, and the same could be true of the Lundy cross.

The Lundy Pony Preservation Society is responsible for the island herd as well as for the larger, complementary herd kept on the mainland.

LUNDY ISLAND PONIES

The predominant colors of the Island herd are cream, golden dun, bright and dark bay. Darker duns and occasional blacks are found in the mainland herd.

TEUTONIC
ROOT

To all intents Germany has no feral or semiferal equine population, and certainly no indigenous ponies like the British Mountain and Moorland breeds. To what degree the wild horses of the Namib Desert are of German origin cannot be established definitively, but without doubt the German connection is a strong one through the early German colonists that settled on the unpromising African coast.

TEUTONIC ROOT

The ponies of Europe are all of ancient origin although their numbers are much reduced today. They carry the genes of the primitive horses of the postglacial period, from which they descend. Konik, Hucul, and Bosnian stock are all examples of primitive descent, in their case from the Tarpan of both steppe and forest; like their influential forebear, they were once wild. So, also, were the two German native ponies, the Dulmen and the Senner

The ponies of Europe carry the genes of the primitive horses of the postglacial period.

DULMEN AND SENNER

These primitive offshoots were the basis for Westphalia's illustrious Hanoverian. The hardy, selfreliant Senner pony ran wild in the Teutoburger Wald to the south of Osnabruck, but is now to all intents extinct. The Dulmen, though much reduced in numbers, lives on in a semiferal condition as a reminder of the wild herds that once ranged freely from the Baltic in the north to the mountains of the Pyrenees on the Spanish border.

The habitat of the Dulmen is still its traditional ground in the Meerfelder Bruch, Westphalia, where a small herd is kept on the estates of the Dukes of Croy near the Dutch border. The Dulmen is, indeed, indigenous to the region—mention was made of the breed in the mid-1300s—but during the last century it was necessary to use outside blood from related Polish breeds, as well as some British stallions, to counteract the effects of inbreeding and to improve the stock generally. For this reason the herd is something of a genetic mix. There is some resemblance to the New Forest pony, but the Dulmen, though a tough and hardy animal, is not so well made as that famous breed.

▶ BASUTO PONY The ancestor of the Basuto pony was the Cape Horse, carrying both Arabian and Thoroughbred blood. It is possible that the Basuto is closely connected to the Namib horses.

The Dulmen's shoulders are inclined to be upright and the neck short, failings that are more acceptable than the generally poor structure of the back and quarters. The ponies are usually just under 13hh. (132cm), and the principal colors are black and brown to accompany the primitive dun coloration with black points and dorsal stripe. Surplus stock is sold at an annual sale, and it has been suggested that some of the Dulmen stock might make useful riding ponies but there is no evidence of the breed making its mark in what is an increasingly competitive field that calls for wellmade ponies of quality. Otherwise the Dulmen fulfils no useful purpose other than to remind us of equine origins.

HORSES OF THE NAMIB

Thousands of miles from the Meerfelder Bruch, in a
country that in no way resembles the horse-raising
area of Germany, there is a herd of feral horses that
shares its home in the arid sand and gravel plains
of Garub with the oryx, ostrich, and springbok of the
southern Namib desert of southwest Africa. These
horses are by no means indigenous to the area, and
there is no suggestion of any German origin, but
there is a German connection from the times before
World War I when Germany had colonial ambitions
in the African continent.

Garub, on the edge of the desert, is an important
waterhole on which much of the Namib wildlife
depends. German colonists built a railway station
here as part of a projected rail system. Today it is
derelict and sandcovered, in the idiom of the ghost
towns of the American West. Indeed, there is not
much left of Germany's brief attempt to colonize this
unpromising coast beyond the remains of the railway,
some decaying buildings, and a handful of place
names like Luderitz, a forgotten town near to
acquiring "ghost" status.

NAMIB HORSES While there is
no discernible type apparent
in the Namib horses, the
overall impression is of well-
bred antecedents, possibly
Thoroughbred/Arabian.

The wild herd—and it is really wild—comprises no more than 200–300 head, the unforgiving desert conditions being an effective control on further expansion. There have been halfhearted attempts to exterminate the horses in the interests of the oryx, but nature, in the shape of the desert itself, is a more satisfactory and less bloody means of control. Today, in any event, the horses, with the other wildlife, are protected by Namibia's Directorate of Nature Conservation.

The habitat is less than hospitable. To the east it stretches over desert to the mountains of the Great Escarpment and from there is subjected to an easterly wind of such scorching heat that it paralyses still further the sterile sands. To the north is the Koichab river, or rather the dried-out bed of the Koichab. Only on the margins of the desert is grazing to be found.

UNKNOWN ORIGINS

There is no doubt that the horses of the Namib have adapted remarkably to survive in this bare, hard land, but where they came from is a mystery and a rewarding subject for conjecture. One school of thought suggests that raiding Hottentots might have introduced them a hundred years ago as they made their way into the empty territories north of the Orange River. If they brought horses with them they would very likely have been Cape and Basuto crossbreds, both hardy and enduring. The Cape Horse derived from horses imported from Java by the Dutch East India Company in the 17th century and was subsequently reinforced by infusions of Arabian, Barb, and Thoroughbred blood. The Cape Horse's importance declined at the end of the 19th century, and it is now represented by its descendant, the Basuto pony.

Nature itself, in the shape of the unforgiving desert, is an effective control on further expansion of the herds.

It is certainly possible that the Namib horses could be descended from the Cape/Basuto crossbreds. They are obviously tough specimens and they display the sort of quality one would expect to be handed on from such predecessors, topped up, perhaps, with later infusions of hot blood, i.e., Arabian or Thoroughbred. And yes, there is the old shipwreck story. It says that a ship carrying Thoroughbred horses from Europe to Australia ran aground near the mouth of the Orange, that the horses made their way ashore and traveled up the bed of the river to the Garub plains. Which begs the question: why not turn right to the more fertile, well-watered coastland of the Cape, rather than endure the privations of a hard journey to settle in a desert with a minimal supply of water and forage? Otherwise, too, there is a lack of supportive evidence of a wrecked ship, which must surely have been recorded somewhere.

Then came the German colonists, and one wonders why they chose this desolate spot. A leading figure in the small community was one Baron von Wolf, who built himself a substantial property on the edge of the desert, the materials being carted across the Namib from Luderitz by ox (not, one might think, suitable animals for a desert crossing). Then the railway was built. At about the same time diamonds were discovered and the building of the railway and the railway stations punctuating the line was continued with a renewed sense of excited urgency. It is postulated that engines and railway stations, which obtained water supplies from underground water sourced by the Garub waterhole, attracted whatever horses existed on the Garub plains because of the presence of the water—which is possible, if only just.

As an adaptation to the desert conditions the horses of the Namib carry little surplus flesh.

During World War I mounted South African troops neutralized the German colony in a decisive surrounding movement. Some horses *might* have been abandoned and others *might* have broken their picket ropes to escape the comforts of cavalry lines for the hardships of a desert without water or feedstuffs. There may have been some horses in the desert originating as a result of Hottentot expeditions or the manoeuvres of South African cavalry; and they may have been attracted by the railway water.

A more likely explanation, and the one that strengthens the tenuous German connection, is the presence of a herd of 300 animals bred by Baron von Wolf and abandoned when that gentleman was compelled to return precipitately to the Fatherland or become a P.O.W. It is this herd that might well have been the origin of the Namib horse. Otherwise, where did they go? They would, too, have been quality animals of the same type as the Namib herd. In adapting to the desert conditions the Namib horse carries little surplus flesh, a common feature in horses exposed to heat, but from pictorial evidence it is clear that the Namib herd is very far from being the degenerate scrub stock that might be expected.

Like the Dulmen, the Namib horse serves no useful purpose in human terms, except that it is a part of our living world, surviving, as yet, without dependence on man.

MOUNTAIN AND MOORLAND

The native, or indigenous, ponies of Britain and Ireland are usually referred to as the
Mountain and Moorland breeds because of the wild upland areas that were their original
habitat. After the disappearance of the landbridges between Britain and mainland Europe,
the breeds were isolated from outside influence for some 14,000 years. It was this
isolation that was a significant factor in fixing their unique character.

MOUNTAIN AND MOORLAND

Given the size of Britain and Ireland, the horse and indigenous pony breeds are disproportionately numerous and unrivaled in their rich variety. The native ponies evolved from the earliest forms of *Equus* and the subsequent subtypes that developed from the primitive root. What is more, this unique reservoir of ancient blood was already established long before the British Isles had become separated from mainland Europe. When the last landbridges from the Scilly Isles, which connected Britain and Europe, disappeared in the Stone Age, about 15,000 BC, the islands and their flora and fauna were isolated from outside influence for a period of some 14,000 years. The only influence remaining was that of the environment itself and so, despite inevitable crossing of particular types at the peripheries, the ponies maintained a more or less fixed character within the areas in which they lived.

The native ponies of Britain and Ireland evolved from the earliest forms of *Equus*.

The result was a unique distillation of the pony types of the Western world, which was enhanced only by the occasional infusion of outside blood made possible after the Bronze Age when boats from Scandinavia and the Mediterranean could be built large enough to carry livestock.

The breeds of indigenous British ponies are thus of incomparable value far beyond their native shores, both as breeds in their own right and as a base stock for crossbreeding. It is usual to refer to the British native ponies under the generic heading of Mountain and Moorland breeds, the title derived from the original habitat of the wild, sparsely populated areas that stretch from Dartmoor and Exmoor in the southwest of England, through the mountainous uplands of Wales on the western side of the country, to the northern dales and fells along the Pennine chain. The rough land of Connemara in the west of Ireland supported pony herds, and ponies were to be found on Shetland and the Western Isles as well as on the Scottish mainland. In the south of the country, in what is now Hampshire, was the home of another native breed running on the moor and woodland of the New Forest. Once the hunting ground of kings, it is still the largest parcel of unenclosed land in southern England.

Today, none of the native breeds is truly feral, although stock is still put out on its traditional range. All the surviving native breeds are bred at studs throughout Britain as well as at studs throughout the world—from the Scandinavian countries to America and Australia. Clearly, the indigenous stock has been refined, or "modernized," by selective breeding and earlier outcrossing, a process that began before the Romans came to Britain.

▶ SHETLAND PONY The original habitat of the popular Shetland pony was the Shetland Isles, northeast of Scotland. Today, they are bred world wide in "domestic" conditions.

The term "surviving native breeds" is used because there were once many more ponies native to the British Isles than the nine Mountain and Moorland breeds recognized today. There were Lincolnshire Fen Ponies, not very attractive specimens but well suited to their wet, marshy environment; there was the Cornish Goonhilly, rough, perhaps, but tough, fast under pack, and enduring, too. Very notable were those swift Irish Hobbys and Scottish Galloways. The Hobby of the 16th and 17th centuries was much esteemed as a hardy, agile animal used by mounted troops and as an all-round traveling pony. With the Galloway, the traditional mount of the Scottish border raiders, it played an important part, via the English "running horses," in the evolution of the world's superhorse, the English Thoroughbred. Then, of course, there was the renowned Roadster of East Anglia, which runs or more correctly, trots, through the equine history of the Western world like a golden thread.

These breeds, having played their part, became extinct because there was no further practical use for them in a changing society, or because they were absorbed by more fashionable equine types, more often than not to the latter's advantage. The Fen Pony, for instance, went into decline once Dutch engineers had completed the draining of the fenlands in the early 17th century, and had probably been in the process of degeneration for some time before. The Galloway was increasingly absorbed into the Fell Pony breed soon after the disastrous Jacobite uprising of 1745, and by the following century it had disappeared altogether.

CONNEMARAS The Connemara is probably the most brilliant performance pony available. It is almost exclusively studbred, although ponies still live out on the moors and bogs of Connemara.

For the present, we are left with nine breeds: Exmoor, Dartmoor, New Forest, Welsh, Connemara, Dale, Fell, Highland, and Shetland. They represent a very special equine group in which each retains a distinctive character and appearance. Additionally, they inherit the hardiness, constitution and sagacity derived from the original environment, and the ability to survive and thrive on the most sparse feed. The modern native pony, however, while retaining those sterling qualities, is a specialized commercial product.

There are no wild ponies, and those kept in conditions nearest to the feral state are now confined to Exmoor, and to a lesser extent to Dartmoor and the New Forest. The ponies of Lundy Island (see pp.109–111) live in near natural conditions but are closely supervised; Welsh stock is turned out on upland moors, and Fell ponies are run on the fell grazing of Cumbria. None, however, can be regarded as semiferal to the same degree as the Exmoor, Dartmoor, and New Forest ponies, which are discussed in more detail later in this chapter.

So why is this equine heritage confined to ponies? And what, indeed, is a pony? A pony stands under 15hh. (152cm) certainly, but the difference between horse and pony is more a matter of proportions. Those of

a horse, which would be over 15hh. (152cm), are long, while those of a pony are significantly shorter. (As an exception, the Arabian, often not standing over 14.3hh. (149cm), is always referred to as a horse.)

The pony's smaller stature makes it better suited than a horse to inhospitable habitats offering sparse feed. Ponies convert food into energy more efficiently than do larger animals and, having a smaller surface area, are better able to retain body heat. As a result they require a smaller intake of feed to remain active and healthy. In addition a small, quickmoving frame copes better with stony, unlevel ground than does a bigger one with a longer, lower stride.

EXMOOR

Of the Mountain and Moorland breeds the Exmoor is the oldest. It takes its name from its habitat in the western part of Somerset, the high, windswept plateau of the Exmoor National Park. It lives closest to the wild state and retains more of the "wild" character than any other. For these reasons and because of its isolation on the moor, the Exmoor has been a useful resource for scientific studies.

Two distinguished scientists, Professor Ebhardt of the veterinary college at Hanover, and Professor J. G. Speed of Edinburgh's Royal (Dick) Veterinary School, made detailed studies of the breed over a period of years and are still regarded as the accepted authorities on the subject of equine evolution. They were able to show a connection between the Exmoor and the equine remains of the Pleistocene period (2 million years ago) found in Alaska. In particular, the unique jaw formation of the modern Exmoor, which has a seventh molar tooth not found in any other horse, matched the Alaskan remains, as did the general bone structure. The trail of these ancient horses, marked by fossilized and semifossilized remains, as well as the evidence of very early rock paintings in the Ural mountains, led through Romania, Austria, Germany and France to the southwest of England, which was then connected to Europe by a landbridge.

The area of Exmoor is one area of high rainfall; it is intersected by swift-running rivers and it abounds in steep valleys known as combes. The vegetation comprises rough grasses and an abundance of heather and bracken. The latter is poisonous to sheep and cattle but is eaten by both the ponies and the wild red deer that share the moorland. They will even paw up bracken and cotton grass in the winter to feed on the starch-filled tubers.

There are three principal purebred herds on the moor, as well as some mixed blood. From the Norman Conquest up to the early part of the 19th century, Exmoor was a royal forest in which local people had grazing rights. In 1818 Exmoor was disafforested and partially enclosed. This policy of reclamation proved to be a landmark in the breed's history, for it was at this point that the two most famous herds came into being. They were formed by Sir Thomas Acland, who founded the Anchor herd (so named because of the anchor brand mark), and John Knight, an industrialist and landowner with a large estate at Simonsbath. The Knights embarked on a programme of improvement introducing a 16hh. (163cm) Dongola stallion, an African horse much influenced by the Barb, and later some Welsh Cob outcrosses. They made little or no impact on the powerful genetic makeup of the purebred Exmoor and passed into oblivion in a short time.

> **There are three principal purebred herds on Exmoor, as well as some mixed blood.**

Of the two herds the Anchor is the stronger influence in the modern Exmoor. A third herd at Withypool, although purebred, shows a variation of type, the ponies being a little bigger and having a noticeably straight profile. The only outside influence on the Anchor herd would have been made through the mystery horse that was given the name Katerfelto. The Aclands recorded that in 1815, before the disafforestation policy was implemented, about 500 Anchor ponies were running wild on the moor and were joined by a dun-colored stallion that was either an Arabian (unlikely, since dun is not an Arabian color), or a horse of Spanish or Barb ancestry. To this day, no one knows where the horse came from, but he was eventually captured and was described as being about 14hh. (142cm) and dun in color with black points and a strong dorsal list (stripe). But since then, there has been no recorded outcross.

In appearance the Exmoor is distinctive. The coloration is bay, brown or dun, a coat color that in the Exmoor is not the expected fawn-yellow but a slate-colored gray, not unlike the coat of the primitive Tarpan. There is a characteristic "mealy" coloring round the eyes, the muzzle and on the inner flanks. In summer, buff markings may appear in the coat, but in purebred stock there is never white hair or white markings of any sort. Indeed, any suspicion of white in the coat or hooves debars a pony from registration in the Stud Book.

◀ EXMOOR MARE AND FOAL
Occasional outcrosses have had no effect on the powerful genetic makeup of the Exmoor and are no longer evident. However, the breed does not thrive away from its native environment.

Stock accepted for registration at the annual October gathering, when the ponies are driven to their owners' farms for inspection and for selected foals intended for sale to be separated, are branded with the Society's star on the near shoulder above the herd number. The left hindquarter is branded with the pony's number within the herd.

Because of its background the Exmoor has developed special features enabling it to withstand severe conditions of cold and wet. It has a noticeably hooded eye (a "toad" eye), an "ice" tail, which has a thick, fanlike extra growth at the top, and a double-textured coat, which gives an entirely weatherproof covering. In winter it is thick, harsh to the touch, and springy. In summer it takes on a close, hard texture, giving the coat a particular metallic sheen. The head is larger in its proportion than that of other breeds. It is suggested that the longer air passages, not unlike those of the Shetland, allow cold air a greater chance of being warmed before reaching the lungs. The pony is robust and well built, and though it stands not more than 12.3hh. (130cm) it is quite exceptionally strong and quite capable of carrying a grown man over the moor for a full day. William Youatt, the 19th century authority, wrote in 1820 of "a well-known sportsman" who rode Exmoors for getting about the country and for hunting, too. The gentleman, who weighed 196lb (89kg), averred that he "...had never felt such power and action in so small a compass." The same man was reputed to have jumped a gate that stood some 8in (20cm) higher than his pony and also to have ridden the 86 miles (138km) from Bristol to South Molton in less time than the fastest stagecoach of the day, and that would have traveled at not less than 8mph (12km/h).

The Exmoor is by nature independent and perhaps for that reason is not entirely suitable for an inexperienced child, but for a competant youngster it is a wonderful hunting pony. Courageous and self-reliant the Exmoor is also a great foundation for breeding bigger horses, either for hunting or competition.

It seems that the sadly depleted Exmoor herds remain as nearly wild as it is possible to be in present-day Europe. In general, their only contact with humans is at the annual gathering in October. Not unreasonably, the ponies are nervous of encounters with humans and even more so with dogs, which are, after all, descended from the predatory wolf, wild packs of which survived in Europe and Euro-Asia until comparatively recent times. Indeed, they are the only British breed that has ever been observed to react to danger by taking up the primitive, defensive "wolf alert" formation: on the approach of a large dog, or even a group of riders, a herd forms a tight circle with the foals at its center. The adults face inwards, presenting a wall of hind feet ready to repulse an attack. The formation, like a well-drilled rugby scrum, then revolves slowly on its axis, while the herd stallion confronts the danger from outside the circle (which protects his rear), ready to attack with teeth and slashing forefeet.

Today, there is concern about the future of the Exmoor. It is categorized by the Rare Breeds Survival Trust as in danger of extinction (i.e. Category 1, "critical"), and it is thought possible that no more than 500 purebred Exmoors may survive worldwide. A contributing factor to the alarming decrease in numbers is the apparent inability of the breed to thrive, or to retain character and type, away from the formative, natural environment of the moor.

DARTMOOR

The Dartmoor pony has always enjoyed a high reputation as a riding pony of above average quality and ability. Today, it is still one of the most elegant of the pony breeds and has movement to match. Unlike most of the pony breeds there is a noticeable lack of knee action, the pony moving with low, long and economical strides—typical "hack or riding action".

Its origin is on the rough moorland of Dartmoor in the far southwest of England, south of the far less accessible expanse of Exmoor. A century and a half ago the ponies were, to all intents, running wild on the moor and were attracting favorable comment on account of their hardiness, their speed and surefootedness, and their extraordinary jumping ability.

EXMOOR PONIES The Exmoor is the oldest of the Mountain and Moorland breeds. Its comparative isolation ensures that it retains much of the "wild" character.

The Field magazine noted that, "they can jump as well as the moor sheep and much after the same fashion, for no hedge or fence can stop either one or the other." It was William Youatt, however, who remarked, "The Dartmoor is larger than the Exmoor and, if possible, uglier." But that was in 1820 and Youatt was otherwise fulsome in his praise of the ponies. (In fact the height limit of the modern Dartmoor is set at 12.2hh./127cm)

Those tough ponies of the old school had almost disappeared during the peak years of Britain's Industrial Revolution when Shetland stallions were put on the moor with the object of producing pit ponies. It was a disastrous experiment that changed the development of the breed irrevocably, but it is from that point that the evolution of the modern Dartmoor can be traced. Today, Dartmoors are bred in studs all over the country. Some small number of purebred stock are raised on the moor and its environs, and mixed stock are also to be found, but the herds of a century ago have gone for ever.

NEW FOREST

A powerful factor in the development of the Mountain and Moorland breeds has been the relative isolation of the habitat, which limited the diluting effect of outside influences. This was not, however, the case with the New Forest pony, whose habitat was open to all sorts of domestic stock that might pass through the Forest on their way to and from the west of England. Before the Norman Conquest of 1066 the early habitat of the breed— if, indeed, so mixed a grouping of ponies could be termed a "breed"—extended across the whole of southern England from eastwards of Southampton up to Dartmoor and touching the fringes of Exmoor. In time, as a result of cultivation, Exmoor and Dartmoor became more or less isolated. In contrast, the huge tract of land in southwest Hampshire, which is the New Forest, became more accessible because of its position on the routes leading to Winchester, then England's capital city, and to the trading centers of the west. As traffic through the forest increased, access became easier and the incidence of outside blood being introduced to the pony herds of the forest became more commonplace.

King Canute's Forest Law was proclaimed at Winchester in 1016, and from that it is clear that the grazing of ponies in the forest, alongside cattle and pigs, was already a long established practice. After the Norman Conquest, William Rufus made the forest a royal hunting ground in which the deer were protected by severe and strictly enforced laws but, for all that, the Right of Common Pasture extended to all those occupying forest land, and this still holds good. The present-day Commoners, to whom the ponies belong, continue to run their stock on the Forest under the aegis of the Court of Verderers, half of which is made up of members elected by the

◄ DARTMOOR PONY In the 19th century wild ponies ran all over Dartmoor. Today the moor is home to only a few purebred ponies and others of mixed breeding.

Commoners. This body is responsible for the welfare and improvement of the forest stock, now represented by the pony herds. It also exercises control over the number and type of stallions running in the forest and carries out regular inspections. The Verderers are also responsible for the overall administration of the forest. To carry out the practical day-to-day management the court appoints three fulltime Agisters. One of the Agisters' duties is to tailmark the ponies; cutting the tail hair in a way that allows easy identification of the districts in which they are turned out.

For a few days each year, the New Forest takes on the aura of the Wild West roundup.

Regular sales of forest ponies are held throughout the year at Beaulieu Road, and for these the ponies have to be rounded up, tailmarked, and branded. These "pony drifts" are organized by the Agisters and carried out by mounted Commoners. They are the highlight of the New Forest year and for a few days the forest takes on the aura of the Wild West roundup. It calls for bold, hard riding on the part of the Commoners and it requires ponies that by experience and instinct can get over the rough ground at speed and that are handy and balanced enough to twist and turn in the pursuit and control of the forest stock. Naturally, the Commoners ride New Forest ponies to the virtual exclusion of all others.

No other breed has been subjected to so much improving zeal as the New Forest, or Forester. As a result of the diversity of breeds involved in the often laudable upgrading of the forest stock it has been difficult to produce a fixed type in terms of height, color and conformational features, although a discernible type is now increasingly evident. Where stock is bred outside the forest in stud conditions, fixity of type is more easily achieved through carefully planned breeding programmes. The best Foresters, indeed, are those that are bred at studs, some close by the forest and others further afield. They excel as competition ponies and are rivaled in that regard only by the brilliant Connemara. However, despite their upbringing and training, they still possess the inherent distinctive character and qualities imposed by the highly pervasive influence of the forest environment. Lord Arthur Cecil, an enthusiast of the breed and a notable improver, called it "the mysterious power of nature to grind down and assimilate all these types [he referred to the numerous outcrosses] to the one most suited to the land." It is also the one as well suited as any other to the requirement of the 21st century for a topclass riding pony.

The first recorded attempt to upgrade the forest stock was made almost 1,100 years ago in 1218 when 18 Welsh mares were put out. Welsh blood was always prominent but Highlands, Fells, Dales, Dartmoors, Exmoors,

Barbs, Arabians, and Thoroughbreds were all involved at one time or another. An early Thoroughbred was Marske, acquired in 1765 after the dispersal of the Duke of Cumberland's studs. His influence was probably not very great since he served only selected mares, but he was the sire of Eclipse, the greatest racehorse of all time. When Eclipse began his remarkable career, sweeping the board in his first season of 1769, Marske was promptly rescued from obscurity and moved to Yorkshire where he continued to stand in surroundings more fitting to the sire of such a prodigy.

The most exotic outcross was a Basuto stallion brought back from the Boer War by the gallant Lord Lucas, the first chairman of the New Forest Breed Society. Lucas lost a leg in that conflict while serving with the New Forest Scouts, all of whom were mounted on New Forest ponies. But one leg or no, he also served in World War I and was killed in action in 1916.

NEW FOREST PONY FOAL
Young ponies bred in the New Forest are well adapted to the environment and develop a special character. They do well as long as their numbers do not exceed the available grazing.

Following the establishment of the first breed Stud Book in 1910 matters were increasingly regularized, although outcrosses were still made until a ruling banning outside blood was made in 1930. As a result the modern pony is in many respects distinctive enough, although there is still a height variation between 12hh. (122cm) and 12.2hh. (127cm), and the maximum height of 14.2hh. (147cm), which is aimed for in studbred animals. All colours are permitted except pinto (piebald and skewbald) and creams of any shade.

The action of the Forester is particularly notable among the Mountain and Moorland breeds and derives directly from the ground conditions of the forest. The best pace is the canter, the one most suited to crossing that sort of moorland. The stride is long and free and the pony is well balanced and surefooted, attributes that contribute to the commercial viability of the breed. While the shoulder is admirably sloped for true riding action, the quarter may fall away somewhat in the forest stock, and the head can sometimes be large and horselike.

Temperamentally, the Forester is intelligent, almost "streetwise," docile, and good-natured. The forest stock move freely around villages, and their regular contact with humans makes them easy to handle. They are, without doubt, less nervous than most pony breeds and perhaps less sharp, or even cunning, than some of the wilder natives. Unhappily, this trusting nature can result in the ponies being involved in traffic accidents, and they do, it has to be admitted, present a road hazard in the forest. In the forest itself, feed is adequate if not abundant, so long as the number of ponies is regulated to accord with the grazing that is available. A principal source of food is the purple moorgrass, which grows round the edge of boggy areas. There is a variety of coarse grass available too, as well as sedge, rushes, brambles, and tree shoots. In season, there are also plenty of gorse tips, which the ponies eat with obvious relish. To consume prickly food of this sort, ponies in some areas have developed "wiry" moustaches on the upper lip and sometimes a rudimentary, protective, beard is found on the lower jaw.

There has been criticism of the forest's management in recent years, much of it justified. The problem is one of too many ponies on too little grazing, and this will be solved only by achieving a conservational balance between the two, and that is a matter for management skills of a high professional order.

◄ EATING GORSE Gorse tips are much appreciated by the New Forest ponies, who often develop a wiry growth round the lips to enable them to cope with the prickly delicacy.

WILD HORSES, MODERN MAN

More humane and caring attitudes towards horses, whether wild or domestic, prevail in the modern world than in past centuries and are, of course, to be welcomed. However, in human efforts to relate to an animal species, there is always the danger of indulging in the destructive practice of anthropomorphism. The horse is not human. It does not have the human capacity for reason. It is a creature of instincts acquired before recorded time and, while it deserves our respect, it is best viewed in that light. Nor, in respect of feral stock, is it wise to confuse conservation with preservation. The former is an exercise in practical management of the environment; the latter, an uninformed rejection of natural fact that is at once sterile and a recipe for ecological disaster.

▶ CHINCOTEAGUE Many of the Chincoteague ponies reflect the strong influence of the Pinto, the principal source of outside blood used to reinvigorate the island stock.

GLOSSARY

Action Movement of the skeletal frame in locomotion.

African Wild Ass The two races of ass, the Nubian and the Somali, from which the domestic ass (donkey)—*Equus asinus*—is descended.

Amble Lateral pacing gait, slower than pacing.

American feral horse Term employed by the American Bureau of Land Management in relation to the Mustang.

Backbreeding Breeding back to specific individuals to produce or retain a particular characteristic.

Barrel Horse's body between forearms and the loins.

Beard Additional protective hair covering the lower jaw. Found in breeds such as the Ariègeois, Exmoor, and New Forest.

Blood horse Thoroughbred horse.

Bloodstock Thoroughbred horses bred for racing.

Blue feet Dense, blue-black coloring of the horn.

Bone Measurement taken around the leg below the knee or hock. "Light of bone" signifies insufficient bone measurement and a serious weakness.

Boxy feet Upright, narrow feet with closed heel. Also termed "donkey feet," "mule feet," or "club feet."

Breaking The early schooling of the horse –. teaching him to accept saddle or harness.

Breed In the wild context: a group of horses of a particular region that, for reasons of habitat or kinship, share characteristics of color, conformation, height, and so on. Otherwise: an equine group bred selectively for consistent character over a long period with pedigrees entered in a recognized stud book.

Cannon bone Bone of the foreleg between knee and fetlock. Also called "shin bone."

Carriage horse Relatively light, elegant horse for carriage use.

Cart horse Coldblood, heavy draft horse.

Chestnut Horny growth on the inside of all four legs or on the forelimbs of asses, zebras, and so on. They are thought to be vestigial scent glands.

Clean legged Without growth of hair, feather, on the lower limbs.

Close coupled Short connections between the parts, particularly in relation to the length of back.

Coach horse A powerful animal capable of drawing a heavy coach. Less refined than a carriage horse.

Coldblood Characterized by heavy horses descending from the prehistoric Forest Horse of Europe.

Colt Uncastrated male horse up to four years old. Male foals are termed "colt foals."

Common Of an animal of coarse appearance, usually of coldblood or nonpedigree parentage.

Conformation The formation of the skeleton and the muscle structure covering it; the symmetrical proportion of the component parts.

Crossbreeding The mating of different breeds or types. Also called "outcrossing."

Dam The female parent.

Deer coat A coat of short, wiry hairs like that of a deer. Found in the Tarpan. It is a "primitive" feature.

Depth Refers to the depth of the body between withers and elbow, hence the expression "good depth of girth."

Desert horse Horse bred in desert conditions, or bred from such stock. Desert horses are resistant to heat, fine skinned and thin coated, and able to operate on a subnormal water intake.

Dished face Pronounced concave facial profile. A distinctive feature of the Arab horse.

Dolichohippus One of the two groups making up the subgenus zebra, exemplified by Grevy's Zebra. The other group in *Hippotigris*.

Donkey feet *See* Boxy feet.

Dorsal stripe Strip of black or brown hair extending along the back from the neck to the tail. Most often found in dun-colored animals. Also called an "eel stripe" or list.

Draft As applied to horse drawing a vehicle, i.e., "in draft." Usually associated with heavy horse breeds, i.e. heavy "draft" horse.

Dry The lean appearance about the head of desert horses. There is an absence of fatty tissue and the veins are prominent under the thin skin.

Eel stripe *See* Dorsal stripe

Entire An uncastrated male horse; a stallion.

Equus caballus *Equus* (Latin), the final development in the equine evolution. *Caballus* is from the word "caballine," meaning of, or belonging to horses. The Latin *fons caballinus* relates to the fountain of Hippocrene, produced by a stroke of the foot of the winged horse Pegasus.

Ergot Horny growth on the back of the fetlock.

Feather Long hair on the lower legs and fetlocks found in heavy horses, coldblood breeds or their crosses.

Filly A female horse under four years old.

Flehmen The action of curling back the lips as an accompaniment to sexual arousal in the stallion. Also occurs in both sexes as a reaction to strong or unusual tastes and smells.

Foal Colt, gelding or filly up to one year old.

Forehand The forepart of the body; head, neck, shoulder, withers, and forelegs.

Forelock The mane between the ears lying over the forehead.

Gardian Keeper of the Camargue horses, the Gallic version of the American cowboy.

Gaskin "Second thigh" extending upwards from hock to stifle.

Gaucho South American cowboy.

Gelding Castrated male horse.

GSB General Stud Book in which all Thoroughbred mares and their progeny foaled in the UK and Ireland are listed. Founded in 1791 and published by Weatherby's, agents to the Jockey Club. All nations engaged in the breeding of Thoroughbreds for racing maintain similar stud books.

Girth The circumference of the body measured round the barrel. (Also the band securing the saddle.)

Goose rump Pronounced muscular development of the croup.

Great game The activities of British and Russian agents in Central Asia in the 19th century seeking to promote and safeguard the interests of their respective countries. The phrase was coined by Captain Arthur Conolly who with his friend Colonel Charles Stoddart was executed by the Emir of Bokhara in 1842.

Halfbred Cross between a Thoroughbred and any other breed.

Hand Unit of measurement used in measuring the horse from the highest point of the wither to the ground. One hand equals 4 inches (10.2cm). The term is medieval, and derives from the breadth of a man's hand.

Harness The equipment of the driving horse.

Harness horse A horse used in harness to draw a vehicle. A horse having harness-type action and conformation.

Heavy horse Any type of heavy draft breed.

Hemionid Half-ass. Not a cross between an ass and something else but an animal that has the nature and some of the characteristics of both horse and ass.

Hindquarters The body from the rear of the flanks to the top of the tail down to the top of the gaskin. Usually referred to as "the quarters."

Hotblood Term used to describe

the Arab and Thoroughbred. Also termed full blood.

Iberian Horse Composite term for the horses of Spain and Portugal: Andalucian (Spanish Horse), Lusitano, Alter-Real, Hispano-Arab.

Inbreeding Breeding between close relatives to fix or accentuate particular characteristics, e.g. mare bred to her own sire.

Light horse Horse other than a pony or heavy horse suitable for riding and carriage work.

Light of bone Insufficient bone below the knee to perform under the rider's weight without risk of strain. *See* Bone.

Linebreeding The mating of animals having a common ancestor some generations previously. It is used to accentuate particular features.

Loin Area either side of the spine lying just behind the saddle.

Lucerne *See* Alfalfa.

Mare Female horse aged four years or over.

Mealy muzzle Oatmeal-colored muzzle. A feature of the Exmoor pony.

Mountain and moorland Composite title for the nine British Native pony breeds. *See* Native ponies.

Native ponies Applied to the indigenous ponies of Britain. *See* Mountain and moorland.

Odd-colored Coat with patches of more than two colors.

Onager A hemionid.

Oriental horse Horses of Eastern origin, usually Arab and Barb.

Outcross Mating of unrelated breeds. The introduction of outside blood to a breed.

Overo Originally an American term describing a solid coat color marked with irregular patches of white.

Packhorse Horse used to transport goods carried in packs on either side of the back.

Paint Pintado (painted). Colored horses. There is an American Pinto Horse Association and also a Paint

Horse Association with differences in registration eligibility existing between the two.

Partbred An animal that can claim a degree of relationship to an established breed; the acceptable degree often being stipulated by the breed society concerned and the stock being eligible for entry in a partbred register.

Pedigree Details of ancestry and appearance recorded in a stud book.

Piebald English/Irish term for a coat of black-and-white patches.

Pinto *See* Paint.

Points External features of conformation. Also relates to color e.g., bay with black points, meaning black lower legs, mane, and tail.

Prepotent Having the ability consistently to pass on character and type to progeny.

Primitive Term used to describe the early subspecies: Asiatic Wild Horse, Tarpan, Forest Horse, Tundra Horse.

Primitive vigor Dominant character and prepotency associated with early wild horses.

Purebred Horse of unmixed breeding.

Quality Refinement in breeds or types usually traceable to Arab or Thoroughbred influence.

Racehorse A horse bred for racing and so usually Thoroughbred.

Rangy Description of horse having size combined with scope of movement.

Roadster Specifically the famous Norfolk Roadster, a trotting saddle horse, ancestor of the Hackney Horse. Also, in the US, a light harness horse.

Roman nose A convex profile found in many heavy horse breeds.

Running horse 16th-century English racing stock of "running horses" that provided the base for the breeding of the Thoroughbred.

Saddle horse A riding horse.

Scope Capability for free athletic movement in a high degree.

Scrub stock Degenerate stock, the deterioration being caused by lack of feed in the habitat, general environmental conditions, or inbreeding.

Second thigh *See* Gaskin

Short coupled *See* Close coupled

Sickle hocks Weak, bent hocks resembling a sickle in shape.

Sire The male parent.

Skewbald English/Irish term for a coat color of irregular white and colored patches other than black.

Solid A coat of a single color: bay and chestnut are solid colored. Also termed "whole" colored.

Sound Of a horse in perfect physical health with no bodily defects and without impediment to sight or action.

Stallion An uncastrated male horse of four years or more.

Stamp A prepotent horse is said to stamp his stock with his own physical character and attributes.

Stamp of horse A recognizable type or pattern of horse, also "a good stamp of horse."

Stud A breeding establishment— a stud farm. Also used to describe a stallion.

Stud book A book kept by a breed society in which the pedigrees of stock eligible for entry are recorded.

Substance The physical quality of the body in terms of build and general musculature.

Tail male line Descent through the male parent line.

Thoroughbred A breed originating in England during the 17th and 18th centuries and popularly attributed to three imported Oriental horses: The Byerley Turk, the Darley Arabian, and the Godolphin Arabian, which were used on the "running horses" kept at the royal studs. The name Thoroughbred first appeared in Vol II of the General Stud Book, 1821.

Tobiano Originally an American term describing a white coat color marked with large patches of a solid color. *See also* Overo

Topline The outline of the back from wither to croup.

Travois A sled designed to be drawn by a horse and made of two poles joined to make a platform behind the horse. It originated in Eurasia and was then much used by (and therefore associated with) the Native Americans.

Type A horse of no particular breed but fulfilling a specific purpose i.e. hunter, cob, polo pony.

Warmblood In essence a crossing of "hot" blood i.e. Thoroughbred or Arab, with coldblood horses, such as coach-type horses, draft horses or ponies. Otherwise, a horse carrying a percentage of "hot" blood.

Whole Of color. *See* Solid.

Whorl A circle of hair on the coat or an irregular formation of hair.

Zebra bars Stripes of dark hair encircling the forelegs and sometimes the hind legs also.

INDEX

Bold face denotes illustrations

ACKNOWLEDGMENTS

Studio Cactus would like to thank the following people for their contributions to this project: Elwyn Hartley Edwards for his encouragement and support; Alison Shakspeare for proofreading; Lynda Swindells for indexing; Tom Butler, Emily Hawkins, Abbey Cookson-Moore, and Aaron Brown for editorial assistance; Dawn Terrey and Sharon Rudd for design assistance.